Other books by Bill Dixon

Another Egypt

The Holy Spirit Handbook

Bill Dixon, son of Ellis and Alice, grew up in Bourton-on-the Water, in the rural Cotswolds, when the sight of a car was a rare thing. He attended Bourton Council School and Westwood's Grammar School, and his first job was at Pulham's Coaches, working in the garage. He later moved to V. J. Colletts and worked on the forecourt and in the workshops.

From 1952 to 1954, he did National Service in The Royal Air Force, as an Aircraft Engine Mechanic at the rank of Senior Aircraft Man. He returned to V. J. Colletts for two more years and learnt about woodwork and felling trees by axe and crosscut saw. In 1957, he left home to train for the Ministry at Bristol Baptist College. He studied theology at Bristol University and served as a pastor at Downend Baptist Church in Bristol for ten years, and at Small Heath Baptist Church in Birmingham for 28 years. During this time he often took study groups to the Middle East.

Bill's voluntary work in Birmingham included serving as Chairman of the Mercian Housing Association and as a member of the Prison Parole Board, and his urban regeneration work in Small Health resulted in a Prime Ministerial visit.

In the 1980s, he undertook a sabbatical at the Newport Beach Vineyard Fellowship, California, led by John C. McClure, who worked with John Wimber and was one of the founding pastors of the Vineyard movement. Bill learnt about the new move of the Holy Spirit and it changed his life. He helped to bring the first Vineyard Pastors from California to the UK.

In the 1990s, Bill began travelling across Africa and took up residence in the black township of Kabalatstane, north of Pretoria, South Africa, where he attended the Truth and Reconciliation Commission hearings. His main ministry was to be in Malawi, working alongside the prolific church planter, Kapalamula Booker Banda.

Bill's interest in Egypt led him to work as a researcher in the Eastern Desert, recording ancient rock art sites under the direction of the renowned Egyptologist, David Rohl. Bill's often humorous exploits in the desert are captured in his book, *Another Egypt*, (Transforming Cities, 2013), with a foreword by the broadcaster and Egyptologist, Professor Joann Fletcher.

In his later years, Bill has continued to travel widely, including in Malawi, Mozambique, Siberia, Iraq, Albania, Lebanon, Egypt, and California, training church leaders and mentoring new believers. In his book, *The Holy Spirit Handbook* (Transforming Cities, 2015), he discusses how the Holy Spirit is moving today.

Bill is a widower. He was married to Jennifer and has one remaining son, Peter.

He now has pretensions to be a poet.

Poems of a Lifetime

BILL DIXON

TRANSFORMING CITIES

First published in Great Britain by Transforming Cities in 2021

Copyright © 2021 Bill Dixon

The moral right of the author has been asserted.
All rights reserved.
Without limiting the rights under copyright reserved above, no part of this publication may be reproduced, stored in a retrieval system, or transmitted, in any form or by any means without the prior written permission of both the copyright owner and publisher of this book, nor be otherwise circulated in any form of binding or cover other than that in which it is published and without a similar condition being imposed upon the subsequent purchaser

ISBN 978-0-9571247-7-6

www.TransformingCities.co.uk

To my Great Nieces,
Sophie-Louise and Amie-Jaine.
You are the future.

Poems of a Lifetime

BILL DIXON

BOOK 1: NURTURE OF THE HILLS

1. Freedom ... 1
2. What is That? ... 3
3. Cows ... 4
4. Earliest Days at School ... 5
5. A Young Boy's War ... 6
6. Double Summer Time ... 8
7. Getting Home ... 10
8. Beside Myself ... 11
9. Well Remembered ... 14
10. Walks For Birds, Flowers and Fruit ... 15
11. Faggots ... 16
12. Calling or Vocation? ... 17
13. No One ... 19
14. Grammar ... 20
15. Westwoods ... 21
16. A Boy's Late Summer Day ... 23
17. Organ Blower ... 25
18. Hidden Truth ... 27
19. The Brown Envelope ... 29
20. Two Long Years ... 30
21. A Story Father Told ... 34
22. What's Your Name? ... 36
23. Getting in and Getting Out ... 37
24. The Right Size ... 42

25 The Shepherdess ... 45
26. Grassholm ... 48
27. The Cotswolds ... 52
28. The Far Cuillins ... 55
29. Accident ... 58
30. Few Love a Rat ... 59
31. Tamo, Lady and Their Labours ... 61
32. Tears of a Father ... 63
33. Encounter ... 64
34. Cotswold Conservative ... 65
35. He Thought He Knew ... 66
36. One for Each of Us ... 67
37. Angels of the Night ... 69
38. Coal Charity ... 71
39. Sling Shot ... 72
40. Came the Day ... 73
41. Winter of '47 ... 75
42. Cage Cleaning ... 77
43. Black Market and Bright Light ... 78
44. LDV to HG ... 80
45. Okay, So You Have Never Prayed? ... 82
46. The Village Bus ... 84
47. Every Family Has One! ... 85
48. Grandmother Knew ... 87
49. Myxomatosis ... 88
50. Dad's Departure ... 89
51. Central Flying School ... 90
52. Mushrooming in the Morning ... 92
53. Crayfish Fishing ... 93
54. Wasps Can Sting ... 95
55. Marks Left Behind ... 97
56. Darkness ... 99
57. The Cress Beds ... 100
58. Strawberry Picking ... 102

59. Tickling Trout ... 104
60. Pulled Over for Praise ... 105
61. Church Secretary ... 106
62. Cotswold Play ... 108
63. Green Curtains in the Sky ... 109
64. Beginnings of 'Lulham' ... 110
65. Moments of Memory ... 111
66. Grandpa ... 112

BOOK 2: LEAVING THE HILLS BEHIND

1. Endurance ... 114
2. Worship ... 116
3. Escape ... 117
4. Theoretical Theory ... 120
5. Church ... 122
6. Science and Religion ... 124
7. Grace ... 128
8. Poetry and Prophecy ... 133
9. Is It Just Me? ... 135
10. Does Nothing Change? ... 139
11. Voice for the Voiceless ... 141
12. Alone in the City ... 144
13. Why is it Monday When it Feels Like Friday? ... 147
14. Compassion ... 149
15. Where Fell the Thirty Pieces? ... 151
16. Majesty ... 153
17. Just a Thought ... 155
18. Gratitude ... 156
19. Laments Can't Hide Truth ... 157
20. Heart to Heart ... 158
21. The White Wolves of Eastcote Grange ... 160
22. Change and Changeability ... 162

23. Confidentiality ... 163
24. Silence in Sounds ... 164
25. Gathering Water Melons ... 166
26. The Ballad of Bay Four ... 167
27. To Think Outside the Box ... 172
28. Babel ... 174
29. Joy ... 176
30. Conundrums of the Future ... 177
31. Precious ... 179
32. A Darker Trilogy ... 180
33. Raining Love in Aid ... 186
34. I Looked Out of My Window ... 187
35. Seeing Leaves in Autumn ... 188
36. Barlow, His Name and Bertha Hers ... 189
37. After the Floods ... 191
38. Morning Movement ... 192
39. Attainment ... 193
40. It's Long (The Nile That Is) ... 194
41. A Requiem for Yesterday ... 200
42. I Got to Think ... 201

BOOK 3: INTO THE PLAIN

1. Behaviours ... 202
2. Winter Must Give Way ... 203
3. Look Before You Lean ... 204
4. More Than an Echo ... 206
5. Conversation Observed ... 207
6. Feelings ... 209
7. Choose Me ... 212
8. There is no Sleep in Night ... 213
9. A Truth ... 214
10. All is Said Through Tears ... 215
11. Here for Someone Else ... 217

12. Prayer ... 218
13. Criticism ... 221
14. A Wedding Gift for the Bride and Groom ... 223
15. Which Direction I Should take? ... 225
16. Inexperience ... 226
17. Rainbows ... 228
18. September Sky ... 230
19. Autumn Watch ... 231
20. Please, Don't Step on My Dog ... 233
21. Surprised by Stealth ... 234
22. A Dream? ... 235
23. The Demise of the Chapel ... 236
24. Wind ... 237
25. Should I Compare? ... 239
26. Christmas ... 240
27. And When the Time Had Fully Come ... 241
28. Season Past ... 242
29. Ode to my Bed ... 243
30. Falling in Love ... 244
31. Yesterday's Poem ... 248
32. Contrasts ... 249
33. Snowflake ... 251
34. Friday Sunshine ... 253
35. Roadside Verge in Spring ... 254
36. Princess ... 255
37. The Bhatia Baby ... 256
38. January Snowdrops ... 257
39. Ella's 'A's ... 258
40. Negativity Fast ... 259
41. Blues Triptych ... 260
42. The Art of Asking Impossible Questions ...261
43. Friday ... 263
44. Trying to Understand Today's Prophetic ... 264
45. Spring Breeze ... 266

46. Today I Saw My First ... 267
47. Why Three Days? ... 269
48. Our Guest ... 271
49. The Ephelumps of Wyndley ... 272
50. Natalie ... 274
51. Feeling Sleepy ... 275
52. Face to Facebook ... 276
53. Inevitability ... 277
54. Return ... 279
55. Pausing ... 280
56. What Might Have Been ... 281
57. English Weather ... 282
58. A Poem for Adam (Bignell, That Is) ... 283
59. Time Before ... 284
60. Expect the Unexpected ... 285

BOOK 4: A FEW CRETAN HILLS

1. Crete ... 287
2. Finding the Right Word ... 290
3. What You See is Not Always What is There ... 291
4. Early On ... 292
5. Above and Below ... 293
6. Agapi Beach ... 294
7. Pomegranates ... 295
8. Date Palm ... 296
9. Pursuing the Heights ... 297
10. Family ... 299
11. To Choose ... 300
12. The Beach ... 301
13. Time Passes, as Does Thyme ... 302
14. Another Day ... 303
15. Feeling Blue ... 305
16. Did They Know? ... 306

17. Maitre D'Hotel ... 307
18. Seen at the Swimming Pool ... 308
19. Dinner ... 309
20. Out of Place ... 310
21. Agapi ... 311
22. The Best of Bars ... 312
23. Gender Behind the Bar ... 313
24. Holidays ... 314
25. Stability and Instability ... 315
26. Name Day ... 316
27. Only in Crete ... 318
28. Sky Watch ... 319
29. Adieu ... 320
30. Changes Seen ... 321
31. Holiday Not Taken ... 325
32. Crete Again ... 324
33. New to Agapi ... 325
34. Vivie ... 327
35. The Life Guard ... 328
36. To Choose ... 329
37. In Praise of Crete ... 330
38. Dangers of Decay ... 332
39. Kreta Cacophony ... 333
40. Times Change ... 334
41. Observed ... 335
42. Now Made New ... 336
43. Holidays ... 337

BOOK 5: HILLS YET TO CLIMB

1. Relaxation ... 338
2. Poor Bird ... 339
3. How to Live Your life! ... 340
4. Appropriate ... 341

5. Noah ... 342
6. Handling the Cup ... 343
7. Flying ... 344
8. Right Divine ... 345
9. Passing By ... 346
10. Sagging ... 347
11. M&S ... 348
12. Sunday at Stow ... 349
13. The Runaway ... 350
14. Well-Chosen Picnic Site ... 352
15. Offers ... 353
16. Taking the Tablets ... 354
17. Ten Dollars is Ten Dollars ... 355
18. Matrimonial Symmetry ... 357
19. A Close Call ... 359
20. Wrong Hole ... 361
21. Time Was Running Out ... 362
22. Blest Rain Upon the Saddest Day ... 363
23. Camping Catastrophe ... 365
24. Harvest Festival ... 367
25. Waiting for Muriel ... 369
26. Motorway Joy ... 371
27. Outlook ... 372
28. Stopped for Speeding ... 373
29. Pop ... 375
30. Lay Preacher's Opportunity ... 376
31. Come to Krasnoyarsk ... 377
32. Here Lies Lenin ... 378
33. The Day the Fish Came in ... 379
34. Spring? ... 380
35. His Pride ... 381
36. Behold the Man ... 382
37. Words for a Worship Song ... 384
38. Good Friday ... 385

39. On Being Eighty ... 386
40. Uncomfortable ... 388
41. White ... 389
42. Peace ... 390
43. Weekend Approaches ... 391
44. Egrets at Eastcote ... 392
45. View From My Window ... 393
46. Home ... 395
47. Courtship ... 396
48. University Hospital Coventry ... 397
49. Cogitation ... 399
50. Taking the Test ... 400
51. A Problem Solved ... 401
52. My Eye Caught His Picture ... 403
53. Swallows ... 405
54. Pic and Mix ... 406
55. Reflections ... 407
56. Seeing Leaves in Autumn ... 410
57. Street Scene ... 411
58. Solihull Café Rouge ... 412
59. Shadowbrook Buzzards ... 414
60. Creed? ... 415
61. Shalome ... 416
62. 'When You Come Together' ... 417
63. Going Home ... 418
64. Did the Supreme Court get it Right? ... 419
65. Wedding Interruption ... 421
66. Black and White or White ... 422
67. Mysterious Fruit ... 424
68. Orlando ... 425
69. Today a Memory Lingers ... 427
70. Elusive Sleep ... 428
71. Referendum ... 429
72. Time Change ... 430

73. Advent's Coming Freedom ... 431
74. Confidence ... 432
75. Advent Reflections ... 433
76. Abstract Pain ... 434
77. I Planted Him ... 435
78. Past Christmas Recalled ... 437
79. Another Year ... 439
80. Outlook ... 440
81. Just Thinking ... 442
82. Tears ... 443
83. Time to Update ... 444
84. Fulfilment not Postponement ... 445
85. An Inadvertent Glance ... 446
86. Our Feasts ... 447
87. Just a Thought ... 449
88. Ask Not of Me... ...450
89. Does it Matter? ... 451
90. What the Dickens? ... 452
91. Thursday Night Through Friday ... 453
92. Running with the Wild ... 455
93. Explosion ... 457
94. Eternity ... 459
95. Tick Box Innocence ... 460
96. Standing at School ... 461
97. Table Top Reflections ... 462
98. Transformation ... 463
99. Liturgy I ... 464
100. Liturgy II ... 468

BOOK 1

NURTURE OF THE HILLS

1. Freedom
(My earliest childhood memory, around two years old).

'Goodnight Son'. The cot secured.
No escape until the morn's release
Would set me free. The night
Was my confinement time.

No point in standing up. I
Could not escape, and looking
Over bars seemed to add
No advantage to the view.

So, lying there, it had to be.
Until the dawn's release brought
Footfall on the stairs and expectation
Leapt within. Another day begun.

Father's strong hand wrapped around
The topmost rail, whilst a finger
Seemed to fiddle with a catch
Below, was all I saw as I looked up.

It was enough, down came the side
And I was free for yet another day.
Lifting me, he gave a gentle shake
As though to say, 'What of the night?'

But I had seen and taken in.
Wanting to hurry to bed that night
I could not wait to be tucked in.
The candle out, my moment came.

Holding to the upright bars
With what little strength I had,
I raised myself and grasped the top
As underneath I looked.

There was the catch. It quickly gave its
Secret up. The side was down. I was away.
No more could cot confine this
Inquisitive young man's mind,
Intent upon escape.

2. What is That?

Running in, I called, 'Come quick.'
And, as most parents do,
No movement stopped their task.
Action that engaged them continued on apace.

Running out, I called again, 'Come quick.
There's something in the sky.'
Standing still, I fixed my gaze upon the
Whispering Aspen that spoke in slightest breeze.

From behind its quivering frame,
Sedate and seeming almost stationary,
The cigar-like shape emerged again as full visibility revealed
Its true identity. R 101 painted bold upon its side!

3. Cows

'Son,' she said. 'Do that again.'
'Do what again?' I said. 'What
You just did, and I will throw
You in that field full of cows.'
I stopped in fear.

For fifty years the fear of cows
Hung round my neck like heavy stone.
Until one day, a cow chased me.
Out of breath, no way to turn, I stopped.
So did she!

The fear of cows was gone.
But what of all those years?
I still would love to know what
Mother wanted me to stop
When in my push-chair bound, I could not move.

4. Earliest Days at School

Janet was her name, though none dared breathe
That truth, for it was Miss and no mistaking it.
Her wrath set fear alight in Primary and her
Word was one to be obeyed, at cost of milk.

Slate boards for learning letters and figures
Forming exercises. 'Collect your card and try
To do the sum. Show me your work before you
Dare to visit the box to change to another one.'

'Today, where do you live? We need you to know,
So when I call your name, just tell out your address.
The number and the road will do, for you to start.'
So it began, and everyone had numbers to recite.

All that is, save me. We had a road. I knew it well.
But of numbers, I had never yet heard tell.
In my mind's eye, I saw our house and on the front,
Above the door, four tile diamonds were set.

My turn came. I called out number four.
No one asked why, most thought I had it wrong.
Today when I pass 'Lulham', for it still stands proud,
I pause, look up, and still can count to four.

5. A Young Boy's War

Tender teens exposed us to subtle snares, as war was all we knew.
Taught and even told to stand,
When King's impediment or Prime Minister's sonorous sounds
Echoed from the wireless, if we had remembered to have accumulator charged,
With HT and LT batteries in place.
Uncertain life, made more certain by their reassurance,
All would be possible. 'When the War is Over.'

The end came and austerity began.
Yet more coupons cluttered purse and pouch.
And with it all the prisoners, German and Italian,
Like Uncles, older brothers, somehow men just like our Dads.
To Chapel they came, and with exhilarating harmony
Embellished carols, giving them new freshness.
Followed by tea and cakes. 'Because the War is over.'

There were those, whose non-attendance was duly noted,
Soon to be forgotten by the fortunate forgiving faces.
The Football Pitch. That was a different matter.
When the local Rovers fielded a full team to face the Enemy,
The usual crowd, augmented by the curious,
Were treated to a sporting battle field.
Here none would yield, you might have guessed.

The penalty awarded looked fair from every point of view.
Herman, for that seemed to be his name, stepped up and placed the ball.

All eyes looked on Larner, the goalkeeper of fame.
Right, left, along the ground, in top corner, the crowd
    chorused.
Three paces back he took, looked at the keeper and the posts,
Then remembered the offence.
All waited a ferocious kick to bend the net.

He moved toward the ball and with the gentlest of touches
Rolled it towards the net, the speed not walking pace.
A cry arose, 'Don't pick it up. Let it roll in.'
Larner didn't, and the cries died down.
Without a score, it was a draw. All seemed satisfied.
Long in my immaturity a question hung.
Should this have been our real war?

6. Double Summer Time

Political debates ensue over a vast range.
But when it comes to time
What could be there to captivate the mind?
It always was, is, and will be.

Yet, in relation to our friends
Whose clocks have trouble synchronising,
We must discuss whether an hour too early, or too late,
Gives light to some, condemning others to the dark.

But can the thoughts extend the days?
Contemplation change what once was deemed sacrosanct?
Alter laws of nature set once for all,
By some far-off divinity, leaving it to run and run?

No. We are only talking of an hour,
Forward or backward, called summertime.
But doesn't the debate go further?
Isn't it two hours now, a double summertime?

Experience is mine, though many years ago.
The war was waging and the farmers needed light
To gather in the harvest; to bind, to stook,
To rick and leave to thresh another day.

So double summertime it was
And I was sent to bed, the usual time, at seven.
No notice of my protestations taken
That it was still far too light.

Then I awoke to the light of dawn, or so I thought.
Downstairs I went, pyjamas grasped
For the tie had long since gone,
Greeting all who were sitting there, 'Good Morning.'

'Get back up to bed,' I hear the stern command
As though it were just yesterday.
'It's still night yet, we'll tell you when it's morn.'
So, up the wooden hill, steps were retraced.

7. Getting Home

Walking always was the way.
Not only home, but elsewhere come to that.
Not always so, says reflection.
The first one to run had to walk,
And he who first walked was carried aloft.
It is memory that tells me so.
After the carrying, came the pram.
One at each end I seem to recall.
The pushchair came next, not for long.
Then it was walking, giving way for more.
But kindness was found in companions
Who, taking the same way as you,
Would call out and ask you to come up.
Up, that was, onto great Uncle Bill's cart,
Which sometimes was slower than a walk.
Then there was Dew Drop.
(His name came from his nose.)
His up was onto a cross bar.
His speed on a cycle soon took you home.
Yet far the best way was the dicky seat
Of the old Bullnose Morris. Markey, the chauffeur
Would sometimes call.
Quickly you stepped up.

8. Beside Myself

The little cottage stood
Beside the weir
Astride the brook,
And bore its name.
Weir Cottage.

Here the footpath
Beside the brook
Began its tour from town,
Overtaking young boys'
Inquisitorial looks.

Beside the fence,
That blocked the way
But let the water flow,
Grew tall thick grass,
A hiding place to show.

And she, beside the fence,
Beside the brook
Beside the weir,
Found in the grass
A place to nest.

I saw it too
On my way home.
Six pure white eggs
Nestling there inside
The grass beside the weir.

One egg I took
And only one. For all
I knew she may come back,
That pure white duck,
And loudly quack.

'Where did you get that?'
When I got home
Was question asked.
'Do I take it back?' I said,
Beside the fire and frying pan.

'No you don't.'
The wise words fell
On listening ears.
'For you may bring but one
A day and she'll be back.'

And so it was
For several days
I took but one,
Beside the fence
Beside the weir.

Always leaving five.
This day there was, but none.
My spirits down,
For that fair white duck
Had, to the fox, fallen.

Now to this day,
Beside the brook

Beside the weir,
When I am passing
I can only think of duck.

9. Well Remembered

Christmas customs, owning endless variety,
Are even found within a cloistered family circle.
Remembered well the Christmas tree, dug up and
Bucket planted, decorated and boldly displaying
Twisted candles, each set in their tiny tin tongs
To hold them vertical, but never to be lit.
All this accomplished, as we slept at Christmas Eve.
Stockings to the mantelpiece firmly affixed,
Before prayers were said and bed bade us sleep.
'Don't hang them up this year, the war is on and
Santa won't be here,' rang in our ears. Thinking
We knew better we hung them up, believing he
Would get through. Alas, morning tears truth told.

10. Walks For Birds, Flowers and Fruit

How we loved those walks: down lanes
Along the river edge; through gated fields;
Climbing banks; exploring dried up ditches;
Hunting through hedgerows; sometimes we
Lay in that pristine plait of countryside,
Calm with beauty. Paddling in the brook with
Oft forgotten soap, to save a wash at home.
Wildlife companions our delight, as nests
(Save those not in use,) were numbered,
Eggs counted, chicks too. And which bird was
That, Dad? The learning process grew.
Flowers, trees, insects, the animals and tracks.
Each had stories to tell our inquiring minds.
The otters where the rivers meet, Windrush
And Dickler that would be, the pheasant's
Feather for Gran's hat, and season's fruit for food,
All had a simple joy to see and gather, as and when.
How we laughed and played and jumped
With joy when we heard the words,
'Do you want a walk today? Which way?
Brick House, Eddie East's Mill, towards
Great Rissie Road, or towards the Camp?'
But the river's meet had my vote every time.

11. Faggots

Not for eating, that would be.
These were the brash, after the
Timber had been corded, cut to
Length, wired in bundles, thick
And thin, for later kindling or
Hearth's fire to keep us warm.

Great Uncle Bill, with his two-horse
Wagon piled high with these wooden
Parcels, trundled down the road,
Turned left through Lulham's
Ever-open gate and to a shuddering
Horse halt gently came.

Climbing onto the cart's timber load,
One by one, he hoisted these bundles,
Flinging them to the ground, making one
Haphazard pile, completing our delight.
For now our work could begin, being
Told to stack them tidy.

Our small hands and arms with
Greater difficulty moved these faggots.
Making dens and tunnels, hiding places
For the games our maturing minds
Would constantly reinvent, without
A screen of any sort in sight.

12. Calling or Vocation?

Too small to sit upon the barber's chair,
Another way was found to spare the man
From bending low to cut the small boy's hair.

A plank was placed across the arms,
All then lifted high. When my turn came, I was
Precariously placed to suffer my tonsorial fate.

My age was seven or eight. His name
And nickname I remember well.
Winfield and Pfoo-Pfoo together went.

The first from parents acquired, the
Second from the Woodbine weed for ever
In his mouth. 'Pfoo-Pfoo,' dispelled the ash.

Between his sucks and puffs, with scissors held
Akimbo, the questioning began. 'What are you
Going to be when you grow up then, boy?'

The answer stunned both him and me, and killed
The conversation from the seated congregation
Awaiting shaves and trims. 'I am going to be a preacher!'

Only God held me to that. Jonah ran away and
So did I. For more than four and twenty years. I wanted
Tarshish. Alas, no exotics, but neither the belly of a fish.

Remembering not what was said that day, I said
'I surrender God. Now please get off my case.

What it takes will not be me but solely You.'

And so it proved to be. Back to school and university
To study things of which I'd never heard. To
Matriculate, graduate and suffer ordination and induction.

It could have been some twenty years in cooking,
For God has a patience that both matches and exceeds
His servant Job. And I, like him cannot lose the questions.

13. No One

Gaffer Harris (all called him that)
The status of Headmaster had.
Blind then, he could well have been.
(For all he saw, or did not see, or did not hear, or did not tell.)
Today, another story would be told.
If what he had allowed should pass,
The system's wrath would fall on him,
Not on the ones given to his charge.

My kindness, if today, would say that he was blind
But, at the time, it was the last thing in my mind.
He must have seen. He must have known.
Yet excuses like 'the war' with ease could well be used.
He, proudly standing, exonerated, pleased
With all the plaudits he received
On Empire's glorious day.

Those left to his and his fellow teachers'
Charge, a different tale could tell.
Bullying and abuse was rife. Calling tears,
Run away and contemplate the ways to end it all,
Occupied the hours no others knew.
None bothered to read the signs, to think or ask.
At tender age, you were fodder for your peers,
Punishment handed down. Who cared?
No one.

14. Grammar

Grammar was a school attained by examinations set.
Only in later years was a name, Eleven Plus, intoned.
One day we went to school to find the desks all rearranged.
In pairs, we sat in solemn, serried rows.

With sternest face affixed and ruler itching to be used,
She summoned us to sit, not talk, and do what we were told.
'Write your name in the space provided, answer all the questions
On the paper you are given, and when you've finished, raise your hand.'

'I will come and check your work.' As always,
Obedient to Ethel, little shivers wound their way
Up and down the spine. She said it, we did it, and
To a fault we passed. She wished us well, we knew not why.

There was an Oral to be passed, but none of us had heard of that.
The day of departure came, we to Grammar, she to
Council and to send a steady stream of erstwhile
Academics to their unknown fate.

15. Westwoods

What was West and what was Woods I shall never know.
Ask me what I liked of the Grammar of distinction and
I'll not tell you now, nor ever will, for there are things a boy will
Keep buried deep inside. And should. The best of all the days
Was the day I did not have to return.

Of course, there were amazing discoveries to be made.
Of girls, of course, and boys. Nothing at all to do with
Academia. So what was here to cause this school to be so proud?
It was Grown Up. So different, with subjects of intrigue
Bathed in fascination and exquisite delight.

Physics, Geography, Maths, not Sums, with Algebra,
Geometry, and English Literature...what's that?
With English Language to dissect and parse. French!
Le Chat et La Rat. I never did get beyond that point
In my excursion into other's language, sparse progress me.

Teachers too were different. They could only teach one thing,
Or two at most. They had such odd names given. Slimy,
Stinker and Hold His Head On One Side. These seemed more
Designations of the pupils, not children. Some were big as grown men.
Intimidating too. Classes became Forms, things called Houses too.

All so confusing, for few came from where you lived.

The local rivalries emerged, surfacing between Stow and Swell.
Unheard of hamlets came to life in prodigies of note.
Sports were taken seriously but best of all, too many boys for
Woodwork meant that Cooking, not Home Economics,
    began for boys.

Confusion reigned when conflicts ceased and folk came home
    from war.
Six Maths, eight French and none for Chemistry,
Teachers did not help the so-called learning process.
Another time of wasted years, as time seemed to evade those
So-called chosen, us, to teach, to prepare for days of hope
    ahead.

16. A Boy's Late Summer Day

Dazzled by the brightness of the sun, dispersed in golden ears of grain
We knew the day had surely come when, from standing tall,
Soon wheat would horizontal lie in its autumnal death.
The harness of the horses made music as they trotted to their task
Down the road, across the path, pausing only for the five-bar gate to yield.
The two brown mares shook and tossed their manes, making
Yet more music soon to be augmented with a consistent rattle
As the binder's flails began to turn in unison by metalled wheels.

These wheels fell silent as they moved from macadam to the turf.
The sharpness of their metal tread moved on to cultivation
For which they were designed, to grip and turn a mechanism of two-horse power.
The binder, for all its beauty, not to make melody its invention.
Far more prosaic its task. First to shear the wheat close to the ground.
Then to gather it into a bundle called a sheaf, secure it tight with binder
Twine. Finally to cast it forth with such disdain, as though all value gone.
Yet round and round the field those steeds toiled on, 'till all that stood now lay.

So, here the work began for boys and men, maids and

mothers too.
The harvest had at last arrived. Standing around that circumnavigating contrivance,
All stood alert and ready to run, to grasp, to rescue, the discarded sheaf.
Sheaves into stooks were built, allowing the sun's summer rays to dry the grain.
Ready for the thresher's art to part the grain and bag it off, ready for the mill.
Boys, always boys, had other thoughts than helping harvest home.
They knew that rabbits ran ever inward in the standing corn. Ready with
Their wooden staves, their job to make sure none escaped to live another day.

17. Organ Blower

Harmonium, that pedal-powered piano, with bursting bags of air,
Having pretensions to be a mighty organ driven by wind trapped
In bellows, ready for its slow-release through keys and combination
Stops, has all the airs and graces of an Ikea flat-pack 'must have'.

On the other hand, that chosen instrument of chapel, church,
Cathedral or civic hall, abounds in manuals, stops, pedals and
A multitude of pipes whose variety competes with Heinz's 57.
Its wind supply by electric power dispenses with the organ blower.

Yes, I have been one of the not-needed in my time. The fund
Began, donations given and soon there was enough to buy an
Electric motor to inflate the bellows and allow the gowned player
To throw a switch, finger the keys and dispense with company.

Reflecting on redundancy, the thought soon crossed my mind.
Reading the black inlaid names upon the ivory stops, a list of
Instruments unfolded, sufficient to make an orchestra.
However,
Here one instrumentalist, with his hands and feet, made up for all.

The chapel in the village filled, each pew packed like sardines.
It was an Anniversary and Sunday School at that. So every Mum
And Dad was there to see their offspring shine, in rhyme and
    recitation.
Yet, without the one who mattered most, could proceedings
    begin?

In his pomp and circumstance, the guest speaker came in. To his
Throne, behind brass curtain rail, the organist took station.
The congregation welcomed, the first hymn was announced.
Alas, as fingers moved the keys, only the sound of silence was
    made.

Eyes to the empty seat were drawn. Who forgot his invitation?
Looking around the assembled host, volunteers were invited
To pump the bellows. No one stirred. The flowing robes were
    seen
To move. The seat was filled and music flowed. The guest
    obliged.

18. Hidden Truth

Beneath the bonnet all the secrets lie, of power and locomotion.
I readily give him this, Father knew my fear and loath of school,
Though he didn't let me know. I lay no fault with him for I don't think
He knew how. He'd had no father to guide his steps in growing up.
The sniper's bullet, at a railway siding in faraway France, robbed both him and me.
Without my knowledge, off to the local bus company, secretively, he stole.

Beneath the bonnet all the secrets lie, of power and locomotion.
'Son, I've found a job for you,' he said, 'there will be no going back to school.'
'Where Dad?' I asked before I let him see a tear I shed, I think, of joy.
'Pulhams, on the buses, or rather in the garage,' he said (with pride, I felt).
'When can I start?' I said, so proud and overcome with excitement.
Monday next was the day of choice, for them that is. I could not rest.

Beneath the bonnet all the secrets lie, of power and locomotion.

So began a journey down the route of all things mechanical.
Taking me to Colletts and on to service for Her Majesty in
Air Force Royal.
Diesel, petrol, aviation fuel, big ends, impellers and Whittle
    engines
(Latterly Rolls Royce), all saw my fingers ingrained with
    grime. Yet,
There was another pull upon my life that would take more
    years to mature.

19. The Brown Envelope

You knew it would, that is, arrive. His Majesty would never overlook,
However lowly the subject was. Duly it came, making no request but a
Demand. Report for medical, education and aptitude test. Tick the box
Marked Army or Royal Air Force: all Navy vacancies are filled.

The dreaded day arrived and the journey was quite long.
Never had I been over the hills and knew not what awaited me.
Train to Cheltenham, then bus to Gloucester, all instructions given.
Do this, do that, sit here, sit there, with never-so-much as 'please!'

Naked we walked and peed in pots; poked and tapped and made to cough.
The soul's humiliation had begun. 'Answer these questions in an hour.'
First six upstairs for RAF, then down below the Army's Pioneer Corp.
'Oh, please let me pass,' an inward cry arose; only dispelled as I began the climb.

20. Two Long Years

Hednesford in Staffordshire; new intakes, raw recruits went heads bowed,
Towards undreamed-of fate or fortune, with no certainty of future. None
Really knew what to expect save those who, through the different Corps
At school had passed. Pay before deductions twenty-five bob, paid into your
Hat each week. Shouting loud, you 'last three forward', you stepped, saluted,
Placed your hat upon the table into which the coins were counted; then collected.
'About turn' and you were on your way to bash the Square. More training hard.

Eight weeks over and a Passing Out Parade. Hold a clipboard. Walk about
Or in the toilets hide. Some unctuous parents came to see their protégé
Ponce up and down the square and wave about the rifles all had been
Taught to use, with and without the bayonet affixed. The bren gun, that was
Quite different. 'Single shot select,' he shouted. 'Aim, fire.' Alas.
To my dismay, I found I'd got it wrong. No signal shot for me but only empty
Magazine. A costly mistake upon the range, using ammunition live.

Home for the '48' then back, to Weeton this time. Trade Training called.
An Engine Mech, my choice. So, lucky me, the very last to be trained for
Engines of all three: air, and liquid-cooled, and pure jet. You could have called it
My element, for these were happy days where I could learn and excel at
Something I enjoyed, without the hassle and the 'soldier stuff' of guarding
Airfields. In those days, no danger lurked and terrorists at work had not yet
Woken. So we slept until the news: 'Officer's inspection car has left the Pound.'

Now a proper Posting came my way, with promotion too. A Leading Aircraftman.
Horizontal propeller now sewn upon the battle dress. 'Aston. Where's that?'
I asked a corporal. He had no idea. So after yet another '48' following eleven weeks,
I found out just where I had been summoned to attend. Transport Command,
A Ferry Unit. Sounded interesting. One old Anson, one old Oxford, with an
Assortment of pilots able to fly the oldest to the newest. Early in the morning,
Off they went to pick up and deliver new planes, from factory to Squadron.

Alas, some days proved too short for all the 'movements' to take place

So Aston became their home, at least for one night,
  sometimes more.
Purposeful, my posting. At least I hoped it so, not as random
  as some seemed.
For beside the ancient air-cooled, ours could be the latest
Spitfire or
Meteor, a Hastings, Valetta, Viking, Vampire or the sparkling
Shackleton
Replacing Lincoln and Lancaster of glory days. Alas the poor
Mosquito, unable
To deploy and lock the undercarriage, looked spider-like
  upon the grass.

Re-organisation, that dreaded word, was feared in those far-
  off days.
Notice of posting duly came, as the unit was run down for
  lack of modern need.
The era of 'pure jet' was dawning fast and Canberra of
English Electric fame,
Sporting two Rolls Royce 'Avon' engines were new for
Bomber Command.
The maps came out to look for Wittering where, in two
  weeks, I would be.
Now, instead of just down the road, the distance from home
  was stretched.
Arrival held its own surprise, a resurrected Squadron with no
  plane in sight.

In dribs and drabs, over the next weeks and months, they
  started to arrive.
WJ720 I remember to this day: my brand new aircraft whose
  engines

Would be my cosseted care, by day and night, until the day of demob.
I got to know my aircrew, visited their married quarters and tinkered
With their cars, all in the cause of being taken for a flight one day.
It worked and invite came. FLt Lieutenant Wilkes threw it around the skies.
Just where we went will remain a mystery, as bucket seat gave little view.

Two weeks after demob, a letter came. I could not conceive why mates would
Write. Did friendship run that deep? It proved to be a kindness
I could have done without. Instead of jovial banter, it bore sadness,
Grief and tears. Just three days after my departure, disaster struck
My plane. A North Atlantic Treaty Exercise took Squadrons to the air.
Alas for mine, the altimeter could be misread by some ten thousand feet.
Into the ground it ploughed, on Scotland's highest peaks. No one survived.

21. A Story Father Told

At the Big House when events took place, the 'hoi polloi'
Were asked to serve. One such was a relative,
Less well endowed with common sense than some.
He had played his part before, outside to wait
On carriages and horses, much less to do with people.

His day did come. Invited in, he stood in awe,
As things he'd never seen before were set upon the table,
Fully instructed what to do when all the guests were seated.
Grace was said. The first course to be served was soup.
Moving along from guest to guest, he ladled out hot broth.

He then stood back and waited as he'd been told,
Until all the bowls were back to pristine emptiness.
Forward now he stepped, as he'd been asked to do,
And to each guest the question put, 'would they like some more?'
Bread and gruel was in more abundance than he had ever seen.

The lady in the black lace shawl, invited to have more,
'Beg Pardon man,' she said and raised her ear trumpet
To locate the optimal position for maximum sound effect.
Bending low, he spoke into the bell mouth, 'More my Lady?'
'Yes please, my man. Make sure it's hot.' came back the firm reply.

Without a moment's hesitation, as she still held
The trumpet to her ear, clearly expecting a reply,
He did no more than pour the contents of the ladle

Down the instrument designed to improve all sound.
Surprise engulfed her Ladyship, and he no more employed.

22. What's Your Name?

The Shooting Brake, forerunner of all hatchbacks,
Was full to overflowing with the holidaying children.
But for the need of petrol, we never would have met.
Mine the task to run the forecourt when none other
Was available. 'So how much will it be today, Sir?' I inquired.

'Just fill her right up to the brim then add it to my bill.'
The reply he always gave. So why I asked, I do not know,
Unless it was in one of my more polite phases. 'Your children home
On holiday, sir?' I said, trying to keep the conversation
Going while the circling smell of petrol fumes engulfed me.

With a considerable sigh, looking around inside:
'This is Jack, this is Jane, this is John, here is
Elizabeth, and this one hiding is Fiona...but who the
Hell are you?' he said, surprised to find another.
'Oh how can I expect to remember all their names?'

23. Getting in and Getting Out

Scattered Cotswold villages bejewelled in autumn sun
Could well remain that way, had not transportation
Intruded on the solitude that still some would not shun.
Horses, bicycles and tractors were the transport's mainstay,
Except for the weekly visits of Fishmonger and Post.

These kindly drivers would take you, free, to where
You fancied for a fee, but getting home was down to you.
Most opted for the mail van. Therein were sweeter
Scents than the odour of the cod and its accompaniments.
Luck was out for her today and Fish Van it would be.

He saw her coming down the path. He knew
Full well, his fate was sealed for it was Friday.
Shopping would dominate the task at this end of the week.
The getting home still puzzled him. Then he realised he was
Worrying about problems that were not his.

A word about her ladyship might help us to move on.
Behind her, seated on the chapel chairs, a more strange sight
I have never seen. For as one person to a chair, for her 'twas
   always
Two. Broad of beam with stature short, her handicap was
   there.
Clear for all to see, it did conundrums cause.

'Twas not her height that troubled him,
Nor indeed that disposition but the vastness of that personage.
Forget the fact this Morris 8 was not designed for four.
With its one forward-facing door, beside her

Ampleness it looked too small for such a mighty deed.

Gallantly he opened it as wide as it would go, being
The only one, yet it still seemed to lack some space.
Reversing in, raising her leg, she made a great attempt
To gain the lowered seat. Then suddenly she let it fall.
Her weight I mean. A noise! later to be explored.

Closing the door, that gentle but reassuring click, absent
This time. Opening it up again, he found it would not shut.
Slamming it harder, to ensure it locked, he heard the
Welcome sound of door secured, but it was drowned
By a shout, as her knee too was put in place.
The winding lanes, leading to the destination,
Displayed that uncertain cloak declaring
Summer was not quite over, autumn not quite begun.
The leaves, reluctant to leave the branches in the breeze,
Were not yet helped by early frosts.

It did not take long, but she only knew of its completion
When they stopped. For looking out from her
Vantage point, only tops of hedges, roofs and sky
Were visible, making no real sense with their
Unfamiliarity and her low-seated posture.

She tried from the inside, he from the out, and
Neither could succeed, in opening up the door.
His vague recollection of a noise returned, that
Marked the quick descent of her largess. Since that time,
Over many bumps along the way, its consequence was
    reinforced.

She, from the inside, he from the out again, with puzzled
Looks from a quickly growing crowd of faces, surveyed
The predicament. What could they do? He pulled.
She pushed. To no avail. The door refused to move or
Release the passenger with kindness and goodwill conveyed.

It had to be his brainwave, as in beside her once again he
Climbed. Just able to release the brake, they moved.
A three-point turn he executed, pointing the vehicle up the
    road.
Ahead a shop, a builder's yard and a house or two.
But more important by far than these, the local garage stood.

On to the forecourt he now drove. That's where I came
In. He squashed the line that rang the bell that called me
To attention, thinking someone had come to buy
Oil or petrol, or perhaps a puncture to repair.
In those days, such was my gainful employ.

'Can you help me?' the fishmonger tentatively inquired.
'What's the problem?' I replied, seeing the distance from
The pumps he parked. Walking over to stand close beside,
He gently whispered in my ear, 'I can't get her out, even if
I could open up the door. I heard a loud noise when she got
    in.'

'Something is broken. We shall need the wheeled jack.
Can you get it please?' I towed it out and asked that silly
    question.
'Where shall I put it?' 'Under door jamb might be best.'
Lying on the ground to check it was correctly seated, carefully
I began to pump and allow the jack to take the strain.

He held the door handle as the van began to rise.
The strain upon his face etched, as the bodywork began
To groan. With a loud crack, that sounded like a whip,
The door gave way and, at last, exposed the passenger, who now was
The attention of another gathered crowd, wondering at the fuss.

Alas, she could not begin to extricate herself for she was much
Too far above the ground for her short legs to reach the floor.
We faced another quandary. All we had so far accomplished was
To open up the door. How could we 'get her out' now occupied our minds.
'Try this,' I heard my boss call out. Even he had left his desk.

Following his instructions, I lowered the jack until the wheels
Touched ground, but just not low enough to take the weight.
To the van's rear doors he turned, asking for help in taking
Out the contents. First the scales, then the bags, to be followed
By the stinking fish boxes that the early train from Grimsby brought.

The sole contents of the van now remained - one large lady.
Still, her egress occupied the advice of all who stood and stared.
My boss had not done yet. Looking at the onlookers,
He found two of seeming strength, putting one in the driver's seat
To push, the other into the back, also to push.

Seeing her forearm was free, he charged another pair to
Firmly grasp and, on the given signal, pull. Now the lady he addressed,
Saying it might prove uncomfortable, as with all her might
She would have to try and escape when some would pull and some would push.
Or else she would have to stay until the van could be dismembered.

Applause rang out as even more stopped to stare
At such a sight, never before in village witnessed.
Free at last, unsteadily she stood, leaning against the van.
Tentative steps were taken until, hurrying along, a lady came with chair.
Only, in the nick of time, to have it snatched away.

Had she sat down upon her sit-upon, with all that weight, the
Flimsy seat then giving way, another predicament would pose.
How to raise her from the ground when no space was left
To push the jack beneath her brave body that had
Already suffered enough traumas to last, at least, one life.

24. The Right Size

Carpenter by trade, calls upon his time could vary.
'Please come, it's very urgent.' Was the message heard?
No phone from home to business. That was yet to come.
As were the many minutia beginning with the brick.

When he arrived, delight swept across her face.
To the smallest room he was escorted
To investigate the scene of the previous night's
Disaster when, lowered to the wooden seat, it broke in two.

It was not the descent that caused the pain,
Rather the ascent: weight caused the wood to part
But then, when weight decreased, the reverse effect
Was felt, as the wood's break closed and caught the flesh.

She said she made a new discovery to add to her list of
Lonely living. None was present, nor within ear shot,
To hear the scream caused as the wooded vice grasped
Only a very small portion of the recumbent meat.

Inquiring if recovery was now sufficient for him
To take some measurements, his mind was wondering how this
Might be achieved without the cause of further pain
To that benighted backside, cushioned now in armchair.

'Have you any brown paper?' he asked, as a plan began to hatch.
'In the cupboard over there, you'll find it neatly folded.'
She was right. Soon, on the cleared kitchen table, paper

Was unfolded. Creases pressed out, he now knew what to do.

'I am now going to ask you to help me if you will,' he mused.
'I'll move this stool close to the table, ask you to climb upon
It, then gently turn and sit upon the paper laid
Out. Then I'll get my pencil and draw a line around.'

'This will then give accurate size and shape for when
It's time for me to carve the seat. This time in solid oak,
I think, as we dare not risk another such disaster.
The old one didn't look robust enough to take the strain.'

'This will be tailor made, with smoothed and chamfered
    edges,
And brass hinges you can polish that will not cost the earth.
No 'ready-made', in catalogues of toilet fixings I have seen,
Would begin to encompass the girth and comfort we now
    need.'

Unstylishly she climbed atop the stool and gently
Turned, lowering herself upon the paper, trying not to
Ruffle it. She settled as some hen might do upon the straw,
An egg about to lay, to be collected later.

Standing before her dangling legs, he reached around
The rear, beginning to inscribe the shape of her anatomy.
Right side first, and then the left, he asked if she could stand
Upon the stool again, thus setting free his new design.

His wife was tasked to press the paper, his brother
Tasked to find the wood, whilst he himself found a saw
And spokes have for the shaping that would later

Lend all comfort to that seat's final form.

Nothing less than hinges, brass, to lend an ambiance
To the least frequented room whose only apparatus
Was designed to do a job which, to all intents and purposes
Should not be subject to either weight or circumference.

25 The Shepherdess

I only saw her once.
Once that is, doing her day job.
'Titled,' some said, as they called
Her 'Lady.' It turned out to be true.
But surely not in that uniform,
As she peddled past our house.
Why do I remember the handle bars were dropped?
The shepherd's crook for crossbar seemed
To change the sex of the cycle with simple string.
With wellingtons that did not fit,
Her dismount was undignified
As she flung her right leg across the bike.
Making no use of the brakes, along its side she ran.
The field next door to us was entered by
A five-bar gate, with some superfluous rope
Wrapped around the post. She had come to
See her precious inmates, a flock of sturdy sheep.
Of sheep seasons, I knew nothing, still less about
The ram, whose later work I learned was
To make a lamb. Disengaging the makeshift
Crossbar now, the crook came into its own, as
This small boy of tender years was about to learn.
The gate made fast, some movement then began,
But only lips and fingers moved. She must be
Counting sheep, I thought, but she cannot be asleep.
To her satisfaction, the first routine seemed done.
Closer to the fence I crept, clearly intrigued to
See what else there was to disturb the
Gently grazing sheep who took quite calmly
To the count, but would be as surprised as me

When the new phase of action began the rout.
What fun this was. Glad not to be seen, and even
More afraid to be heard, out loud I laughed.
With feet in floppy wellingtons, she began the chase.
The object seemed to be to catch a sheep
But only in a certain way. That day I was to learn
Why shepherd's tool was called a crook and why
The shape and for what task. She ran along
Beside the beast, firmly grasping crook by handle
And in a flash she caught the first and, with deft
Motion, flicked it on its back. With legs all flailing
In the air, I saw the tool enclosed the hind leg's knuckle
Not allowing for escape. Its day had come.
Helpless. In country parts, as we grew up, to
See a sheep upon its back, all must be stopped.
To the rescue you must run and set it on its feet again
For very soon, in struggling, it will die,
Unable to upright itself without your helping hand.
So why had she done just the opposite? To
Disable it, of course, for now the real work could begin.
Not now in shearing pose this season, but holding it the
Same, she seemed to be searching through the
Wool. True it was. She was looking for the ticks and
Lice that live and lay their eggs upon the skin
Beneath the wool, and breed. Some potion she applied
And when at last her work was done with one,
After the next she ran. So it was that every individual
That day was scrutinised for sickness, disease and
Malady. One thing hung unresolved in my untutored mind.
How did she know which sheep was done and which needed
To be done down to the last: when all were done?
As childhood gave way to youth, and youth to

Something else, first I was told and then I learned
That there was One, whose sheep I was, who treated
Me the same; who knew which one I was and my own
　　malady;
Who daily, or more frequently, would immobilise and
Administer such remedy, tailored just for me; set me
On my feet again and let me run free. In dotage still
The picture haunts. Her 'Ladyship' his Lordship doth
　　enhance.

26. Grassholm

The island, from the naked eye
In distance can be seen, as
Standing on Skomer's western edge
You look across the tranquil sea.

From the mainland you set out,
Named St Martin's Haven, leaving
Your car secure and safe in the National
Trust's car park, patrolled by whiskered one.

His jovial greeting would begin
Weather forecast for the day
And the wisdom of your attempt
To reach both Skomer and Skokholm.

For Grassholm his wisdom was not
A little guarded but as 'The Princess' skipper
Was ready to set out, we trusted both
Him and his fellow navigator.

It long had been a dream
To see the distant white, into the
Multitude of gannets, merge: to sail
Down wind, avoiding guano smell.

As we approached a most amazing sight
Of heaven on the move with extended wing.
So we looked up and failing sky to see, we heard
The sound of sea and wing-beat making symphony.

Around this upheaval of rocks, almost
Reluctant to escape the sea, we gently cruised.
The muffled engine spluttered now and then
As all failed to see the fast approaching mist.

Enveloped in moments between those rocks,
'Which course to steer' became a captain's choice?
Sending his jean-clad mate to fetch the pole, she
Pushed with all her power, reversing us.

Completely clothed in damp grey veil, our fate
Began to form as a question in our mind.
Ship-to-shore communication with earnestness
Began, as still our navigation from the whirling pools

Struggled for the open sea. Clear, he thought,
And, throttle forced, the boat began to surge with
Proud prow lifting from the water, suddenly
To stop. All was thrown in disarray, as we hit rock.

Encouraging us, the captain said the hull was
Double skinned. We would be safe, no need to fear.
The only trouble was, currently he had not
The slightest clue as to where we were.

Near to the cabin seat, I slid and saw
The bright array of instruments displayed.
Then it was I heard the conversation and went cold.
'When the needle stands up straight, is that the north?'

As though to reassure, he said a distress message
Had been sent. Someone was sure to come

To rescue us at some time but he had no idea
When. Rocking gently on the swell, all heard the sound.

Minutes passed as eyes tried in vain to penetrate the
Fog to see if sound would be transformed
Into shape, to save the day for us. Of necessity it
Would have to come quite close if we were to see.

It did. We saw. Towering above the smallness of
Our vessel, a fishing boat held station. Its
Captain looking down on us saw us look up at him.
Fear in our eyes but fun in his, we did not appreciate.

He called our captain to show himself, asking
Politely if we would like to be escorted to the mainland.
I, with the handful of passengers, felt a surge of relief
But that was premature, as captain to captain had more

To talk about. Discombobulated, we could only wait
And listen to their exchanges as they shouted to and fro.
The gist of their debate was this, that nothing would be
Done until our captain confess that he was lost.

Protestations followed on, for ship-to-shore
Communications would also hear his sad confession
Which for a captain lost at sea, surrounded
By three modern navigation aids, would mean all

Would know his predicament, and not again could he
Walk tall, with head held high, back at his yard
In harbour secure. 'Tell him you're lost,' was the
Passengers' advice, 'and let's begin the journey home'.

Eventually the plan was put in place. The fishing
Boat turned and, ensuring we were in its wake, the
Tandem slowly moved ahead. What had been planned
Adventurer's day turned out all expectations to exceed.

27. The Cotswolds

Such an evocative word is Wold. Now
Add to it Cots, it's even more so.
History and etymology will, without
A doubt, allow a discovery of sorts.

Stone sheep shelters linked to
Rolling, tree-covered hills, of
Ancient cultivation, reaching back
Several thousand years, gives Cotswolds.

But that is not the road down which
I want to travel. It is to touch the very
Ground beneath my feet, allowing
Them to press out something of the past.

The ploughed fields yield up their
Sea urchin Oolitic limestone fossils,
Life was there long before the
Sapiens of Homo-species walked them.

The streams and rivers gently flowing
Through woods and forests, long since
Thinned and almost gone, provided
Our forebears place, space, and nourishment.

Evidence abounds of those who
Went before, as modern motorway
And mega-store disturb the sleep of soil's
Secrets, buried, not far beneath the sod.

Poems of a lifetime   *Book 1*

What shaped these hills to give
The drapes which enfold us in their
Welcome and hold us in their strong
Embrace that tells us we belong?

Mellow, warm and workable that stone,
Quarried for centuries, to wall and roof
The dwelling place of those who were
Held by the sheer affluence of the hills.

Taken far away as well, to build the
Nation's pride in Cathedral glory, both
Here and in antipodes. Near at hand, so
Many colleges of Oxford owe, too, the debt.

Asked what it is that brings me back
To the place where I was born, I would
Find it hard to say, for in my core being I
Have never left the soft beauty of Bourton.

Venice of the Cotswolds, sometimes called.
Shops come. Shops go. Names change.
Locomotion moves ahead, as transport
Changes with the passing of the years.

As age allows for memory to be selective,
Silence affords more than moments
To recall. Often a slight scent triggers a
Moment far lost in time that excites the soul.

Such is one: a walk to where the rivers
Meet, Windrush and Dickler, to make one flow.

Where otters played and crayfish were caught.
Birds too. Ah, to find the Jay's covert.

The food and fruit these hills provided
Helped to keep us alive in days of war,
When 'Lord Haw-Haw', would predict the
Destruction of the CFS, Little Rissington.

Now the venue of the tourist, in vast
Numbers, from the most far-flung places
Come to see what has, and is, moulding a simple,
Yet in many ways a proud and profound people.

From gathering little fossils from ploughed fields,
Or gazing down from high escarpment,
To looking at landscape, close or distant,
Is to discover the rich greens and gold of Nature's gifting.

Mist, ice, snow, rain and fog, each
In turn, wrap round the landscape, changing
Its appearance as they move through
Season's sequences, seamlessly and always silently.

With one voice the rolling hills are calling, in many
Varied volumes and inflections, to any who may listen:
 'Come, and share an ancient glory,
 Gifted by Creator, called The Cotswolds.'

28. The Far Cuillins

Kyle of Lochalsh to Kyleakin
With no bridge in those far-off days,
Took us to Skye, of mountains high and vales.
We circled now the Black Cuillin's peaks, these
Which were our call and goal.

Watching, as they changed their shape
With every few yards that we drove.
Looking always to our left, we fell to
Wondering how high we might climb,
When Loch Brittle calm gave way.

Letting the light of the morning paint
From its dawn palette ever changing shades
Of gold, purple, yellow and of green,
Whilst we checked and rechecked
Pitons and ropes for an earlier start than some,

The gentle slope of Glen Brittle called
Us both to look up and look back.
Before us the mountain's beauty,
Behind us the blue of sea, pulled at heart's
Exploration, today or the morrow maybe.

The spell of those black mountains drew us
Ever upward and onward, till ropes were
Attached, in the first place to waists, then pitons
Examined for later implant in the rocks,
As we inched our way up higher.

It was then we glanced the blueness
That day the sky displayed. It was,
However, not at the colour we looked
But for the source of noise, of
Aircraft not seen yet drawing close to crash.

Louder and louder grew the noise, as
Hearts beat in synchronised fear
That airliner of some vast proportion
Would, with the mountains, collide and
Change forever delights of day.

When no plane could be seen, the range
Of vision changed. Looking up, yet
Only as far as restrictions allowed,
The unexpected overtook us. There, rolling
Over high peaks, grey mist turned to a fog

Shroud, through which the anger of the
Mountain peaks began to spit their tiny
Fragments of splinted rock. In a moment
The scene changed. Guns of the Wild West roared
As their bullets ricocheted around the rocks.
Then, out of that grey blanket, tumbled
Stone. Then rocks, in size increasing to those
Of boulders, then of cars, and then of single
Deck buses that grew to proportions of a
Double Decker. Fearful, we clung to rock

At the same time destroyer and saviour.
Looking down across our shoulders, we saw
This tumbling mass strike other rocks and

Smash below some that had settled their
For years, never expecting to be disturbed.

Late afternoon saw two shaken climbers
Back at the camp. After the ritual
Divestment of climbing gear, tentatively
We made our way to the local hostelry where we
Sought a place, as far from people as we could.

The long cool evening passed in a convivial way,
As those whose expertise and local knowledge
Far surpassed that of ours. We listened and
What we heard, such story did unfold, that to this day
Belief is still suspended that we walked away.

'I saw that rock, whose instability caused me to
Raise my binoculars for a clearer line of view, just
As it toppled over and down. With a mighty crash
It tumbled onto Boiler Plates and shattered in
A thousand fragments, cascading down the gorge.'

'But listen that was not all I saw, for clinging
To a rock, I saw two guys with ropes.
When all the dust had settled and the noise
Had ceased I looked again, and they were gone.
None could have survived that avalanche of rock!'

Huddled in a corner we listened to our fate
Recorded by these seasoned men whose one
Delight in life was to ascend those mountains black
And be among an elite band who, finding joy
In dizzy heights, gained satisfaction from the peaks.

29. Accident

With careless abandon he drove down the road
That would take him to his home and his family.
So too was I, on the same journey bent.
Alas, he did not signal the right turn he executed
To enter his drive. That was the moment I chose
A perfect, passing manoeuvre.

Down he drove me, and my motorbike.
I lay there bleeding from a leg, as helmet
Saved my head from contacting curb.
Sounds I could hear, in distance seemed,
Growing louder by second. A siren for sure.
Then a voice spoke, very close to my ear.

It spoke of the need to exchange details.
At first, in confusion, I did not hear.
Until a small card was thrust into my hand.
For a moment I wondered, had he plundered my pocket?
It was then I saw what had made me perplexed,
For twixt my card and his, only road name

And number differed from each other.
Our forenames and surnames were identical,
With symmetrical symmetry, even an A between.
He to his home, to tell a tale.
Me, in the waiting Ambulance, to hospital
Taken, where my tale to tell would have to wait.

30. Few Love a Rat

My car had sat on the driveway
For two weeks of holiday. Time now to fire
The engine into life once more, to release movement
To its muscles, and get it moving once again.

The switch was switched, the engine turned
Spluttering into life. Or so I thought, for all it could
Do was to splutter and splutter again. To the
Well-trained ear, it was only firing on two.

Investigation under the bonnet was an urgent need.
There, nestling between rocker cases, lay the half
Chewed carcass of a discarded chicken dragged here
During twilight hours by, yes, you guessed, a rat.

Feasting on the bones however was not enough for him.
Taking another bite, he bit into the plug-lead
That had far richer taste. To my horror, I could see
Were he had sharpened his teeth, to my disadvantage.

But dislike of rats began when, as a boy, the chicken
Feed he stole. Recourse to remedy could have been a
Fierce terrier, owned by some near neighbours, yet
That involved freeing flagstones under which he hid.

So, on that day I saw him play (I always assumed it was
A 'him') not yet knowing whence the fresh supply
Came, that so readily restocked those of which we disposed,
I quietly crept indoors and called my Dad to get his gun.

First standing still, we then advanced side by side
Towards the door that led out to the garden at the back
Used as front, except for those very special days,
When, for some reason I never understood, front was front.

Looking through the open door, we watched him play.
The gun was broken and two cartridges inserted,
One to each barrel,
Ready for discharge. No-one, save me, saw the postman
    coming.
'Don't shoot!' I shouted very loud. All lives were saved.

31. Tamo, Lady and Their Labours

He, the large and proud one, Tamo.
She, the quiet, gentle, graceful Lady.
Everyday both fed and pampered,
Sometimes in the house, more often
In their cages.

Come Saturday, cages opened and down
Into the darkest depth of a deep sack,
Though still separated, as becomes lifestyle,
They were slung across the back, wriggling
On the way to work.

Down the lanes and through the hedges,
Destinations beckoned; hunters to the hunted.
First, the nets were disentangled.
Having first been made and mended
In the fire-lights glow.

Find the holes. Securely net them.
Look for the bolt, some way away.
Now is the time to release Tamo.
Line and collar attached, adjusted,
As nose is shown the hole.

A quick look round. A sudden rush.
He disappears into the darkness. His line
Through fingers run. Now and then, he pauses.
Gently putting tension to his exploration
As he pursues his goal.

Stand still, but not to listen, rather feel
Through feet, the pounding beats deep
Beneath as prey rushes on until, quite suddenly,
One net is taut against its peg, bouncing as its
Captive freedom seeks.

Lady, still nuzzling round the sack, needs
Neither collar nor a lead for she, unlike her
Fellow operative, will never be distracted.
Single-minded, pursuing the racing would-be escaper,
She could catch it.

Some days she would hunt for Tamo,
When he had gone astray in labyrinths
Beneath. Sometimes she would hold his prey.
Then the reason for the spade we brought was clear.
We dug them out.

The hours passed as the day's harvest grew.
High above the warren, on convenient branch,
The rabbits hung, awaiting retrieval on
Journey's return. So, to a close, came another day
Ferreting to feed the family.

32. Tears of a Father

Only once, in his short life of five and fifty years,
Did I see my Father cry. The papers came. The call
Went out. To muster, if you were fit, to fight the foe.
And Dad was off, early in the day, to make the many miles
Where doctors, with their accoutrements would test each
Thing that bent, or in some special way articulated, but
Only to perfection. 'Breath out. Breath in. Pass water
In this pot. Stand up. Bend down. Now cough. Take this
Paper over there and do as you are told.' Yet what
I haven't said, as yet, is the parting from his Mother.
He could not consult with Father proud, who once had
Volunteered, for all that there was left of him lay
Buried in some far-off field, in far-off country where
He had met his death. A sniper with some accuracy
Curtailed his life and left his Mother widowed.
No, I do not believe it was revenge he sought, but
Just to say to mother, for his name and honour, I
Will go and try to help to do what he did not.
In the room, as he came home, I saw it all myself.
Up to the table, he pulled a chair. Sitting down,
He rested elbows on the cloth that even now hung down.
Burying his head in his hands, he sobbed and sobbed
Again. 'I cannot go, they won't let me go, they say
That I'm not fit to go to face the foe as father did
Before. Mum, they said I cannot go. How can
I be left behind?' The rhythm of his sobbing shook the
Table top. Ashamed, I think he was.

33. Encounter

Do you remember it? That first moment when death no longer was a word.
That moment when it became a living reality. 'He's gone', the hushed words
Said, that I was not supposed to hear. Who's he and where's he gone? My
Mind began to whirl. I was seven and so was he. I was, and he was not. Ah,
That dead. Like when we kill and eat a rabbit. When the trap is sprung and
Mouse is dead. Or when you crush an ant or let a spider know his days are
Done. That dead, when someone comes to take away a body I know not where.
His name was John, and we were sad, but dreams that night were bad.
For the very first time, as I recollect, I began to wrestle with what death
Was. Understanding, such as adults might bring, was lost on me.
My memory says I thought he was happier than me, but it was dark and I could think.
Could he?

34. Cotswold Conservative

Walking home from school,
There was no other option I admit,
I saw a big posh car pull up.
Quite a rare occurrence here.
A man got out.
All in the street stood still.
First a ripple, then a roar,
Applause echoed all around.
Folks were gathering in groups.
I gazed. I'd never seen the like.
'Who is it?' I enquired.
'Why don't you know, boy?'
They all chimed. 'That's our MP.'
I should have asked if
Any, by chance, might know his name!

35. He Thought He Knew

Though only young, I knew the day the General Election came.
It coincided with a visit from the Family Doctor, in his car, to visit Gran.
(Much to the surprise of all of us, as there was no medical necessity.)
She was all dressed up as though to go somewhere and indeed 'twas true.
He had only come to take her to the polling booth, like all good Conservatives do.
Now the choice was clear for either. It was to be Mr Churchill or Mr Attlee.
Winston or Clement, Conservative or Labour, all knew the way
The Doctor would cast his vote. Yet, if he thought a ride in his posh car
Would cause Gran to do the same, he was very much mistaken.

36. One for Each of Us

LDV to HG, Corporal to Sergeant,
Through the ranks my Father moved.
Indentured as a carpenter and wheelwright,
His skills gave every man a gun, albeit wood,
For drill and ceremonial duty.

The day did come when the Enfield 303's
Of standard issue were deployed.
Ammunition, to begin with, blank.
Live rounds eventually were delivered.
I recall the hours spent filling magazines.

Almost seven years of war passed slowly.
But for Dad's Army there was much fun,
As I can well attest, for now and then I
Joined in, playing soldiers. School was where
It hurt, as dead father's names were called.

In later years, we found again the gun.
Handing it in at the local Police Station,
We were asked where the ammunition was.
Promising we would look, we found a biscuit
Tin containing magazines and many rounds.

Yet there was more to come. Secretly
Hidden, where only Father knew,
Just seven rounds, separated from all
The rest, put to one side. A thought. Our family
Comprised just seven of three generations.

Had invasion taken place:
Had the foreign troops come near:
Had the enemy approached our door:
Father did confess, seven dead they would have found.
For there was one for each of us, and one for him.

37. Angels of the Night

Straight ran the road before the many bends would bring me home.
Darkness was pierced by a shaft of light sending a beam before the roaring
Motorcycle, seeming to chase, in some great race, the brightness before.

Suddenly ahead, but in opposite direction, new beams fought against the dark.
Clashing with the single strobe, the driver's consequential blindness for a moment
Caused concern. Dipped headlight switches on. Two beams lowered and one went out.

I harshly braked. I had no sight, only a blaze of light ahead. I could not see.
Then the oncoming car drew close, turned off its lights and stopped.
Of what was I afraid, as a faint moon illuminated two figures approaching me?

Their hands were holding things unseen and my heart began to race.
As they drew close, I thought I got a glimpse of screwdriver and pliers.
Without a word, they had my switch apart. Wires disconnected and rebound.

Wired to the dipped position, wrapped in insulation tape, I had a beam.

Before a word of thanks my lips could escape, they had turned around.
To their car, they went, got in, shut the doors and pulled away.

In minutes, only one or two, they had disappeared. My engine into life I brought,
Engaged the gear, let out the clutch and with a surge straight on, set off.
From that day on to this, I do not know. Angels of the night? I am a believer now.

38. Coal Charity

The coal men came, shoulders bent with weight of fuel.
They saw the heap of slack and tipped their sacks.
Shaking, folding, gathering them up to go for more.
Then their one mistake was made. They took no notice of
 her.
The small shaking form, with hands on hips and glowering
 gaze,
Said, 'Ignore me at your peril. I've ordered none,
Who said bring coal?' was her demand.
'The British Legion, Rose,' they said, 'it's a
Gift for all War Widows, approved by the Committee.'
'Don't call me Rose. Bag it up and take it back.
Tell them what I said. In all the thirty years of widowhood
They never thought of me before so, if they think
That I'll accept their charity today,
They have another think a-coming. Bag it up, take it back,
Get off my land and take your coal elsewhere."

39. Sling Shot

He tried his best to teach me. Accuracy, he called it.
Said not to make the same mistakes he made.
'First time,' he said, 'I missed him.'
'Second time, I hit him, but alas in the same place.'

40. Came the Day

If I could put it in one word, it would be
Awe. There is the overworked addendum,
Awesome. No that does not this truth tell.

From rolling hills and long tradition,
From the Vale of Bourton's beauty,
From the education of rurality,

To the city, to the College,
Was there really only one?
To the hallowed Dinning Hall and Library,

Not yet a chapel with its acolytes.
All yet to come and more. Awe of
Champion, and Dakin, and all who'd been before.

Awe of fellow students who seemed to know so much,
But that was probably the first bubble to be burst.
Awe tinged with fear: a shared room for a start.

Westbury-on-Trym. Now where was that?
With Carlyle Litt, was that his name? J. B. Middlebrook,
Of BMS fame and then Bristol Role of Honour, awe.

August men and places all met on day one.
Now Bristol greats left for us first years, on day two.
Trepidation tried to trample on the awe.

This building with its electricity and showers,
Unheard of at home. Its pictures of past presidents,

Yet, on the upper floor, 'rouges' gallery displayed.

Too old to shed a tear, too bold to be put down,
It all began with awe for me on that warm September day.
Still to this one, awe it is, that claims an ageing heart.

Awe now that, in God's purposes, He lead a way.
Uncertain still, when Canaan called, I only made Haran.
Time is His, not mine, and still the beating heart's word is
    'awe.'

41. Winter of '47

We thought we had escaped but it was not to be.
Late February and early March, the snow began to fall.
Each day it added depth and new shapes began to form.
From huge iced cakes and prehistoric monsters to
Fragile icicle and patterned leaf-lace hanging.

At night, a frost preserved each shape to have
Its corners chamfered by the morning sun until
New falls of snow festooned the trees and hedgerows.
Soon all semblance of the known was lost in unfamiliarity.
Coldness invaded every cavity as frost froze all.

Birds, unlucky to alight upon a momentary thawing
Branch, found themselves frozen to the perch. By
Morning they were dead, frozen balls upon the trees,
Lacking only fairy lights to turn them into festive scene.
And still the snow was falling. 'Snow on snow,' we sang.

The first to venture forth cleared a shallow path and
Sprinkled ash, to prevent the slips and slides parents
Abhorred but in which we children took great delight.
Next day, the depth of snow was dug again and sides began
To grow in height, so high there was no seeing for a child.

Paths with high walls became passages along which we
Ran, to road and outside loo or chicken-run to feed the frail
Birds that magnified themselves, fluffing out feathers,
Making them appear twice their normal size. Unlike
Their cousins in the trees, they were to survive the cold.

Relentlessly the snow continued its downward descent,
To the delight of youngsters, whilst fraught parents
Wondered when all this would cease. Theirs were the
Cares of food, and fuel. Ours the fun festivities.
Sometimes too, there was little meeting of the minds.

Domination of the trees was soon no longer extant,
As snow by dint of depth turned their tops to bushes,
Whilst the bushes disappeared, gaining length
As whipped up by the wind, vast swathes of drifts altered
The landscape and blocked the roads, making all impassable.

Snow ploughs, the size and shape of which we
Had never seen, were augmented in their work by
Prisoners of War who manually dug, defiantly, great cubes,
Stacking them like pyramidical blocks awaiting some
Vast construction project, in the whiteness of the frozen
    waste.

Then the thaw began. All fun stopped in the dampness,
As water began to find a way to escape its frozen
Belly. Unsuccessful in its journey, to sink in soil beneath
Or flow towards the river, which had begun to flow again.
Floods were the next great enemy, finding no place to flow.

He came through floods and piles of dirty snow.
His mission to find out why four children had not been
Attending school for several weeks. It was plain to see,
But apparently not to him. Soon, however he was to learn.
'Get off my land. If you can't see, then I can't help you.'

42. Cage Cleaning

Uncertain as to functions pets perform,
For a country boy it seemed they had to
Earn their keep. Exception came with a
Canary whose tenure, even in his cage, did
Not last long. He sang in sunshine so was
Hung outside. My task was to clean the cage.
He saw his chance and as his seed and water
Were replenished out of the larger holes,
He flew to freedom, to sit upon the fence
In shade or sun to sing, and I simply disgraced.

43. Black Market and Bright Light

With Double Summertime holding at bay descending darkness,
No concessions to time were countenanced, even though
Oft debated with some passion. Some hostility of 'why?'
Triggered parental ire. Children had to climb the wooden hill.

So off to bed it was, but sleep? Some long time it be feigned tonight,
For it was Friday. That night when, if anything was going to happen, it
Would be then, for sure. And if, as we were often told, the Germans
Were on their way, then surely down the road, on a Friday, it would be.

Softly she whispered through the blackout's darkness across the room,
'What can you see?' as, quietly, I pulled the heavy curtain back
Just far enough to see, through the small panes, what might be
Happening in day's dying light, as we held station in artificial night.

The Morris Eight Van drew up beside the gate and my report began.
'I can't see who he is, but I can see Dad opening up the rear door.'
'They might be tea chests but for sure they are big boxes and

they're
Coming in.' Clandestine visitation issued in, for us, yet more
    Cornflakes.

44. LDV to HG

The epaulette said LDV and Dad explained that he had volunteered.
The Medics agreed his health was poor but we all knew his heart.
If he could not go, then he would stay and do his part for king and country.
The Local Defence Volunteers had nothing, save the village pecking order.
Doctors precede Bankers, who precede Shop Keepers, who come
Well before the artisans. Last come labourers, 'of farm' being at the end.
So the ranks were thus distributed and rural hierarchy upheld.
But father held a trump card. How to defend the homeland without
Armaments? That's where the carpenter's skill came to its own.
Each member of the Little Rissington Platoon was well equipped.
All paraded and performed their drill impeccably, displaying ability,
Each with his hand crafted wooden Lee Enfield 303. Whilst
The Carpenter's son was the proud owner of the only Tommy Gun in town.
Father soon advanced the ranks. Lance Corporal to Sergeant,
Defying all long established countryside conventions, where each his station
Knew to whom to doff his cap. Then the Home Guard came, replacing

LDV, to be the grand equaliser that destroyed all class and privilege.

45. Okay, So You Have Never Prayed?

A young boy's pride, as Father gifted him a watch.
Its twin hung from a chain, leaving it always hidden
From all prying eyes in his upper pocket. Never
Marking much, save time to start and time to stop.
But then again, all marking for moments were there.

What is there in a boy that sparks that nature
Of inquisitorial intent, that must leave all in
Constituent parts, one day to be put back in place?
Around the house lay many bits awaiting the great
Day of grand reunion, when all would be rejoined.

Secreting the small screwdriver hidden in PJs,
I stole up the stairs and soon sat on the bed.
What urge drove me to try and gently prise the glass
Front that protected face, big and little hands?
Candlelight seemed very dim but eyes were young.

Breath could be held no longer and its exhalation
Blew the candle out. The screwdriver slipped and,
Until the match was stuck, results could not be
Ascertained. It was the ears that gave the hope as
Sound of falling cover heard, as it hit the boards.

The light revealed the truth and the wish within
Was that it would not. Alas, in commotions fury,
Both glass and hands had parted company but that
Was not the real catastrophe. The bright white
Enamel face now bore a vicious gouge, a jet black scar.

Thoughts cascaded through the pale yellow light, as
A sifting process was begun. The best solution had to
Be found, and fast. The hands and glass replaced, the
Prayer began its formulation in the mind, as only faith
Could match the dire needs of the hour, or second.

So a deal was struck. My understanding was for it
To work, there had to be two parties in agreement.
But there was only one, and that was me, which meant
That I had to stand in for God as well. Placed under
The pillow, come morning and the repair would be complete.

That, of course was God's part. Plain for all to see.
But what, to clinch the deal, demand would
Be made of me? A 'quid pro quo' had to be found with
Some alacrity. For my part then, promises and promises.
What I would not do, if He would mend the dial by morn.

46. The Village Bus

The country bus its tortuous route pursued.
Down twisting lanes, up steep-sided hills, all
Among the Cotswold's beauty, stone walls
Delineating the depth and field of view.
Into the village, it wound its way to collect
More passengers, town-bound to find the weekly
Victuals. All windows that would open were.
Now heads began emerging, as the motor's
Motion slowed and to a standstill came.
'Twas then the local wit gave voice to his
Wisdom of the day. Raising it above
His queuing comrades, shouting loud,
'Put thee 'ead in Missus, or they'll think it
Be a Cattle Truck.'

47. Every Family Has One!

She was wacky, she was wild, she was witless, she
 was mild.
Her love of life was visiting, whether she was welcome; left
 others wilting.
Any numbers of families have them but try to secrete them
 away.
Uninvited, unexpected, without a knocking they will enter.
A pall of desolation falls upon the home. To whom does she
 belong?
No one will admit. Long since has passed the day when
The children ran to bear the news, with excitement, 'Guess
Who is coming up the path?' Now they, in silence, slink away.

Talk! Could she talk? It was a wonder when she stopped.
From whence the habit came, no one could tell.
One theory said she had been brought up a lonely child,
That was discounted when her siblings were counted,
Some twelve in all, as folk could remember. Others
Said, in whispered tones, some had gone missing.
Another theory was advanced that said she talked
So much because in reality, had she not, no one would have
 heard,

There again it was a boys world in those days too.
Assertion in extended family is given to some.
She was clearly one who, at any cost and none, made her
Presence felt, particularly to the fit and young who at least
 could run.
But, getting back to talking, she never let a subject deter her.
You could not say she was an expert, but voluminous

Shallow information can often pass for competence.
She had of course lived long enough to have outlived most.

On family affairs, she proved it, going off in all directions
Through countless generations, the skeletons in cupboards
Encountered were numerous. She alone delighted in them,
To the shame of captivated audience: they wished her frequencies
Could be less. To make offence was only matched by her ability
Not to take offence, for to listen to the voice of others was a gift she was not
Given to show. As in one departure, her kindly host was heard to say,
'Do please come again when you haven't got so much time.'

48. Grandmother Knew

I stand before his resting place
Reading Name and Rank.
A thousand miles now separate
My home from his.

It was his age that caught my eye,
In years, of course, a youth.
He a mere eighteen or so and me almost eight-o.
A mere six feet of soil, our separation now.

Yet, I can turn my head and see,
Whilst his skull now, always stationary.
For what great cause had he come here to die?
And what has brought me now?

Here I stand and catch the tears,
For I am the one who sees
All the intervening years,
Whilst he forever rests.

49. Myxomatosis

Mid-fifties, in the mind engraved
Images of animals in countryside of death.
We, on our Sunday afternoon walks,
Twixt Young Men's Bible Class and Evening Service,
Determined the need for stout sticks to
Dispatch the diseased and dying population.
Rabbits have the reputation of prolific
Breeding, but death came faster than
Their ability to multiply in the decimation.
Deliberately caused, to control?

50. Dad's Departure

Dad's departure, caused by directing labour
In the deep days of war, brought about
Another unexpected household change.

Now, out of seven, six at full roster left.
Gran, Mum and the siblings, four.
Alas for me, alone the man, of only years eleven.

He said, "Step up and be the man; you I leave in
Charge." Recounting responsibilities
As evening came and darkness fell, I was transfixed.

The house had to be secured, all locks and bolts
In place, then the blackout checked.
Demands of the morrow meant today's task was set.

Sitting on the stool, polish and brushes in place,
Five pairs of shoes regimentally lined,
For Gran's were only brought out for occasions special.

It was done, simply, because it had to be.
No compulsion, Dad did it, so I did.
Relief at his return was a new emotion learned.

51. Central Flying School

Up the hill, a mile or two at most, lay the CFS.
Its designation Little Rissington or, locally, the Camp.
A training station for ambitious pilots to enhance the sky.
A source of economic wealth to villages in the time of war.

In many pies, he had his finger set, my Dad's employer.
Local entrepreneur. Builder, market gardener and bowler
For the local cricket team. Slow spin, with deceptive hand
Change in approach, foxed many a foe at Bourton Vale.

So, for him, my first job it had to be. Lock up the turkeys
Every night, in case the fox might come and find me wanting.
For half a crown a week. I looked and wondered why anyone
Would want the acre of cabbages through which I had to
   walk.

'You coming with me to Camp?' he called as I went to
Collect my pay. Having never seen inside the perimeter fence
'Yes,' jumped out before I thought. The boot-door of the
Vauxhall opened, enabling us to fill it full, with cabbages.

Laden down with produce, and the steep hill ascended,
Before us was the main gate, which to enter needed Pass.
What it was, I do not know but now we were inside and of
All places, at an airfield, the NAFFI we approached.

When all arrangements had been arranged, the car
Now devoid of all we brought, was turned around.
A homeward journey and not one plane I'd seen.
Such disappointment to a boy who dreamed about the Camp.

The skies above echoed every day to Harvard engine
Screams. Others, of both later and earlier vintages too,
Created cacophony above all day. The silence became
That to be treasured by us below, who knew it all must be.

52. Mushrooming in the Morning

Ah, to go mushrooming in the morning, that was joy.
Over stiles and through the hedges scrambling
To where we knew the horses had been.

What they left behind in steaming heaps, so I was told,
Made for the perfect womb where spawn could
Germinate and thrive, creating what we sought.

Yes, you could collect the buttons and their more
Open elder brothers. But what we sought, through the
Crisp morning air, was just one that would fill the frying pan.

53. Crayfish Fishing

Walking along the Windrush river banks,
You would not guess what lay beneath
The shimmering surface of that clear water,
Between the quivering reeds and yellow King Cups.

We were neither there for tickling trout,
Watching water vole, or sighting the slithering
Otter's silvery twists and turns, nor
Dragon and Damsel Fly, flickering in the light.

Weeks have passed as preparations made.
A circle of metal clothed in chicken wire,
Then three strands of stout string join to
A long extension, of some yards' length.

With broom handle modified with steel loop,
Through which the coarse thick string
Could pass, and with deft swing across the
Dazzling surface be swung and lowered.

Whence must come the bait? What better
Than a trip to the fish shop and ask for,
'Five Cod's heads for sixpence please,' and
Come the evening, set out across the fields.

When all was set, we sallied forth to exercise
Our skills. Father first, to show the way, then
Children followed on, trying to land the traps
Close to the banks in stiller, shallow water.

Watching now, all twelve were set and we to wait.
No shadow to be cast over the glittering sheen
As we walked back along the lines, hearts
Beating faster in anticipation of a catch.

Without a sound, yet subtle movement made,
The pole, with loop along the string, silently slid.
Then, with lift and thrust and swing out onto
Bank, there before us lay our anticipated haul.

Willows watched and heard the plops, as some
Fell headlong back to the water's safety.
Whilst those detained, ten or a dozen at a time,
Into the safe keeping of a big brown sack were thrown.

Waiting 'til all was safely stowed and
Homeward way begun, the conversation
Turned as to where we might keep our quarry,
Also, just how to cook this crustacean.

Wending our way, arrival came. Home at last.
A sack, three parts full, of noisy crayfish
Crackling claws into the bath were tipped
To await the second fall into the boiling water.

What a feast for family supper. Something
Quite new. Now bright red from funereal grey,
Cooking complete. The claws were sucked and
Tail meat chewed, as tired feet were rested.

54. Wasps Can Sting

Winding, the Windrush wended its way through the meadows.
Broad banks built diving-boards, for boys to display their skills.
Running, we rushed to be first in the cooling water's evening heat.
Finding fun in simple things, first past the post, portended.

It stood in an innocuous hole; pause and you heard the sound.
Bass buzzing, suggesting there may be thousands deep beneath.
As you passed, you stirred the stick. That raised the octaves high.
Alas, the last to pass might get a sight of what lay hidden.

Yes. I was the one. Emerging in their thousands, the willow of
Wasps massed over me. In moments, I was clothed by them
Trying to sting my clothes. I could not guess how many. It was my
Face, exposed, where I would count the ones that penetrated skin.

Twenty-one, all down right cheek before I brushed them off,
Pierced the skin, implanting their chemical bile to burn in me.
As I ran, the cloud above blotted out the evening sun, following
My every stride. Ripping off my garments, I plunged below.

Under the water little was to be seen but, as I surfaced,
A raft, a moving mass of gold and black, floated downstream.

Following the briefest of swims, until stillness and silence
Settled once more across the field, I scrambled out and
Dressed.

55. Marks Left Behind

Fingerprints and DNA cannot belie the truth we passed that way.
With intention, or unintentionally, we leave a trail, hallmarks of our
Being here or there, for others following to find and read a story.

Often, as a boy, I stopped and read my name in raised lead letters,
Standing proud against the white hewn stone of memorial stature.
What did he do? Where did he go? They say he only volunteered.

But slowly, for the pain did never pass, his wife, my grandmother,
Put together for me snippets of his past. And yet, I longed for more.
I'm glad I did not promise - but in a way, I wish I had - to visit his grave.

Another day came when we laid his son, my father, in the grave.
Both were far too young to die. So now, I look around the village
To see what he might have left behind. Some mark to stamp his passing.

And there it is for all to see, talking to each visitor, as the wind
Makes hinges speak, welcoming and pointing out the way

they take
To see the Model Village. Yes, he made the post and sign. Others planted.

The roof, rafters and gable ends, of varying pitch for each
    building,
Were his handicraft as well, before their being transported to
    Hank's
Quarry, where stone slates were added. Then, pristine. Now,
    weathered.

56. Darkness

Not only was the night dark to the child
Who, in the midst of war, walked to school.
Daytime, too, was deep darkness in the
School air-raid shelter, on practice day.
Or when 'Dare' was played in the Pill Box.
Two encumbrances were Gas Mask and Survival Box.
Putting one on had to be practiced weekly.
Yet, only once a year was the other opened,
Its content an Aladdin's Cave of confectionary:
Biscuits, bars of chocolate, and sweets.
One we wished to lose, the other forever keep.

57. The Cress Beds

The clear spring-water flowed over polished gravel.
A veritable breeding ground for water cress.
To pick it was to steal, so we never tarried there.
The bed ran round the double-bend, then on, down the
    straight.

The motorcycle and sidecar had intention too,
To take the bends and then go down the straight.
Alas, it was his trial run. He did not make the bends.
He went straight on down the bank, in among the cress.

Help was at hand. No ambulance or nine, nine, nine.
Rather, a passing shepherd on his way to tend his sheep.
Seeing the plight, he turned aside and, with unhurried
Step, walked up the long drive to the big, thatched house.

He pulled the rope that rang the bell. Pulling again,
And yet again, for in these rural parts response is slow.
From around the back, a gaitered hand sauntered into view.
'It be another in the beds. You make the bed. I'll get 'em out.'

So they went their separate ways, one to fish the fallen
Out of cress, the other to bring out the bed and set it up
Beside the road, but in the drive, to lay the injured
Out. M'Lady brought the bedding and made up the bed.

About an hour had passed. The shepherd to his sheep
Returned. The motorcyclist and sidecar passenger in an
Iron-formed double bed reclined, in the middle of the drive.
Whilst the erstwhile hand wound his weary way, doctor

bound.

M'Lady made the tea and broth and the Master tied
The umbrellas up in place, as the passing shower had
Made the invalids twice damp. You're right. It was a
Familiar task, as frequently folk fell into beds.

58. Strawberry Picking

Nights drew out, as in the countryside we said.
School soon out and bikes left to hand.
The word was out. 'Wood's strawberries ready.'

Off up the hill to Clapton and through
The five bar gate, into the field's long
Furrow-like mounds of strawberry plants.

Hiding among the leaves, reddening fruit
Looked bashful in the sun. 'Go get your punnets
Then start here. Work carefully up the row.'

On hands and knees the search began
For the ripest fruit. Soon the first container
Was filled to overflowing and set aside.

Maybe, for full thirty yards, the rows
Ran up the field, yielding now to little hands
Their choicest fruit fit to sell at market.

Back down the row, you gathered as you
Went, each piled-high punnet, fitting
The first dozen into the waiting crate.

Next, the weighing process. Scales set
For one imperial pound. You hoped to have
Enough from your twelve to fill some more.

Sometimes a surprise was yours, as
Hidden on the ground was the nest of the

Sky Lark filled with four or five bright eggs.

But best of all, by far, was when old Isaac 'ood
Come accounting with his book. 'It be threepence
A punnet for thee.' I clung to the ten-shilling note.

59. Tickling Trout

It was another boy, about my age, who showed me how.
To take the wired waste bin from the tree.
To kneel beside the water on the river bank.
To cast no shadow across the sparkling sheen.
To wait with patience for the shimmering silver trout.
To gently lower the hand, breaking the surface smooth.
To agitate the gravel, muddying the clarity. Then suddenly
Thrust up and throw the cage, and fish behind, upon the
 bank.

60. Pulled Over for Praise

The cones created mayhem.
Confusion reigned supreme.
Which lane, of three to choose,
Became a single country track.
Carefully I manoeuvred giving
Others a little space. Blue lights
Flashed. Arms were waved. Pull
Over, stop, the indication seemed.
Mother-in-Law sitting next to me
Was puzzled by the fuss. She was
Not alone in that. Alas, I too feared.
'Is there a problem Officer?'
I ventured to express.
'Yes Sir there is, but it has
Nought to do with you.' Surprised.
He went on to explain.
'To get the one behind, I had to
Pull you over. You are to be commended.
But the Book is being thrown at him.'

61. Church Secretary

Cecil, with his white moustache and beard,
His white wing-collar and stiff black suit,
With faint white stripes, called pin,
Stood erect before the assembled host.

Sunday School it was, not the cake shop of
Each Saturday with sixpence for a pie or cake.
And he, supreme, looked down upon his scholars
Who looked up to him with awe and admiration.

Wilkins was a family name that had a reputation.
The Mill, the Bakery, and Shop all bore that
Name with pride, but Chapel was the prime
Contribution to the village life of Bourton.

Before the Romans came, spanning the Windrush
With Fosse Way, the Dobunni tribe of Celts, a
Settlement of size and status giving birth
To Bourton, from far off days preceded them.

History, for all the truth it has a habit
Of revealing, needs to be joined at some point.
The seventeenth century is my place, when
Dissenting soldiers of Roundheads passed through.

Not alone, these upright men came carrying
Their Bibles. Tradition has it that they met
Those with eager ears to hear the contents of
Their faith and creed that was so controversial.

Dissenters were born among the hamlets of
North Cotswolds and the village was its focus.
Sixteen-fifty, or thereabouts, the pundits say
To celebrate the Baptists. So, to this day, they do.

No longer is the first sanctuary there to view
But round it the ancient cemetery still remains.
There Cecil had his resting place marked out
In the mound remaining from the demolition.

Boxbush, his home, once guarded by five-bar gate,
Stood central. All knew he lived alone, but never
For a moment lonely. In his death, he decreed a
Stone gatepost should mark the spot for you to see.

So by some quirk of fate or coincidence Cecil was
Laid to rest at Salmondsbury's Ancient British Camp.
This one time conquer of the Matterhorn was
From height brought down to dwell with history.

62. Cotswold Play

Seasonal green and autumnal shades of Bourton Vale
Today hide, in enchanted beauty, the once wide expanse
Of meandering water that left behind the rich alluvial
Deposit of golden gravel: such nourishment for farmers.

Now confined within the banks of Dickler, Windrush
And Eye (somewhat latterly embellished with hamlet,
Village and isolated farmstead), such rivers and streams now
Provide pastimes for visitors bent on Cotswold exploration.

But to such, born and bred in this ethereal paradise,
The more mundane discovery beneath the fertile soil,
Came about through play with spade and bucket. No
Seaside excursion, saved with Sunday stamps, needed.

What boys, and girls for that matter, did not enjoy the
Delight of digging holes, just for fun, when through first
Layer of soil, then second, that of gravel was achieved?
The third brought new dimensions into play: water.

Clean and clear, through gravel strained, we made our
Own streams and puddles in which to jump and splash.
Such fun, when all we had to do was to pretend. We could
Be anywhere in the world in our Cotswolds' mind's eye.

63. Green Curtains in the Sky

Voices were raised, footsteps sounded on the stairs,
Doors rattled. Something of import had to be happening.
We were supposed to be asleep.

'Get up, now.' The command rang through the house.
'Come down at once, this you have to see. Follow Dad.'
We were supposed to be asleep.

Out of bed, we scrambled; down the stairs, we tumbled.
By the 'Only to be opened on a Sunday' front-door we left.
We were supposed to be asleep.

Into the darkness of the garden, in flannelette pyjamas,
Letting the wind have its chilling way where it will.
We were supposed to be asleep.

'Look up, look up,' commands still echoed round the garden.
'Can you see them, the green curtains in the sky?'
We were supposed to be asleep.

There they were, emerald green drapes, touching the horizon.
Stretching from far distant apogee, so rarely beheld here.
We were supposed to be asleep.

'Aurora-Borealis,' father said, whose word was never doubted.
Next day, at school the Northern Lights were mentioned.
No 'suppose' about it. We were asleep.

64. Beginnings of 'Lulham'

Miss Reynolds owned the land and Uncle George the money.
With Son in Law a builder all the signs were looking good.
But the year was in the twenties and she a single Mum.
To fence the land, to find a mortgage, then build a home
Would need determination, stubbornness, and courage.

Foolishness, some have said, as to the train station drawn,
To the city, where banks and building societies abound.
The field was fenced and chickens bought, for eggs and
Meat, all in good time. Financing with potential she told
The account advisor. So new to them, a woman at the helm.

Many more things would be new to them by the time that
She was through. What's your problem was a question put,
Along with the assertion that it was their job to find the
Cash. Then came the master stroke as from her handbag,
With a flourish, she took, the War Widows Pension Book.

65. Moments of Memory

Such fascination, turning page on page.
'Strange but True', the title said, as a fly
Was shown to stop a locomotive by a
Direction change. Silly and impossible.
Familiarity with trajectory would later
Come as I was seven and more schooling
Lay ahead.

Today I watched a spider and had recall.
That same publication had declared that
His web is stronger than steel of same
Dimensions. Could that really be true? I
Found myself inquiring as I watched in
Glowing admiration his ability to span
Vast space.

But inward turned the thinking from
Flies, spiders and antics of impossibility.
What I cannot see between me and thee
And often it, is that which all cannot exist
Without. The air we breathe, existence
Maintains for all that is alive, save that
Water bound.

66. Grandpa

Waiting, the line in which he stood was long,
As had been time spent for the day's arrival.
Hiring Fairs were said to be nearly over and this
Could easily be the last that Stow would see.

They came from many Counties wide, to buy
The horse and hire the man. Then meld the two
In Farrier fettle and they would seek you out,
Hire you on the spot and give a starting date.

Still in his teens, from Naunton he had come
Where father was the local Chimney Sweep.
Into service on a grand estate his ambition.
Horses were his passion with all their needs.

From Madley, Shropshire, the boss came, to find a
Willing hand. Seeing young William, in his teens,
He knew he had his man and took him home to
'Lulham', there to mould the boy into a man.

So later William took Rose, his bride from Bourton,
And at only 18yrs they married at the Parish Church.
Then together they worked the seasons round.
From ploughing to harvesting and seasonal hop picking.

Before the house the boundary Haha gave a view
That did not let the live stock too near the tidy
Garden. Still to be seen today but the new reputation
Is for 'Lulham' wine, bringing new prosperity.

War interrupts. So it did for them. Raising two
Children, off he went to use his Farrier skills
Again, this time in France, until the snipers
Bullet left Rose a war widow and single Mum.

So when then new house was raised beside the
Rissington Road there was only one name that
Came to mind to capture and retain all the
Memories of young love. 'Lulham' came to life.

BOOK 2

LEAVING THE HILLS BEHIND

1. Endurance

Can darkness gain more darkness yet,
And is light doomed to the same fate?

Is this a truth black holes teach,
Or was it yet some rumour?

Tomorrow's darkness, drawn to today,
Joins the pain and torture of the past compressed into the 'now'.

Is 'now' that bottomless pit, into which is poured
Unfettered darkness of emerging light and the night itself?

Yet, to Him, the opposite is true.
'Darkness is as light to You.'

Yet again,
'Clouds and thick darkness surround Him.'

Where can I go from your Spirit?
Where can I flee from your presence?

Obstacles of thought pile high across the path.
Paradoxes of Almighty abound, cradling the questioner.

Who am I that I should presume to question him?
Still the fool, who once believed he knew and understood.

Now a wiser fool who says, 'Enough!'
Content to be a Job and let the questions come.

Knowing that to stand is all that is required.

2. Worship

God has filled the World with music and the means to make
 it.

When music caresses words,
Inside a transformation takes place:
A new reality is born and I am changed within.
He stands before me, invisible in light
Yet defined by years of friendship, forgiveness, and my
 unfaithfulness.
No words invade the space between us now,
As they are lost in melody, not heard with ears
But with the heart and mind.
Now I know as I am known.
The work of Grace, expressed in Mercy,
Reaps its reward in life: in Him, I am alive.

Heart discloses heart, without the need of words.
Love's unity has done its work.
The longed for is a present possession,
The dreamed of is procured.
The asked, received before the question formed.
Then the descent, where feet touch ground again.
Eyes opened, three dimensional sight restored.
Needs abound every which way you look.
Hold back the words and let the strong embrace talk.
Tears will flow, disclosing a reflection of His finding space in
 you,
Shared, for it is all you have to give.

3. Escape

Contemplating escape one day
As I sat with the prisoner in his cell.
It was impossible to see
How, if ever, he would be free to escape.

The door was locked. All I had to do was knock.
And he could knock forever.
Other places of confinement crept across my mind,
With equal obstinacy of exit.

The past seemed first contender for paralysis and prison.
It contains, confines, constrains any forward impulse,
Entrapping you for decades with walls and bars unseen;
Stronger than the high tensile steel and concrete, reinforced.

'I can't, I couldn't, I'm unable,' make for bars.
But walls are made of sterner stuff.
What my father, mother, teacher said, powerful
    pronouncements,
All without a shred of truth, yet cemented strong

To curse my cowering spirit and direct its encapsulated
    course,
Leading me nowhere, forever to be the slave.
Every ambition, hope and destiny aborted before birth.
'Wretched man that I am, who shall deliver me from this
    body of death?'

Then Churchmanship creates a cage that sees all outside
Contaminated with what cannot be thought as wise,

seemingly or sound.
The sphere of truth contained within is only really truth to
   me.
To you your truth, though true, to me is not my truth.

Now forever in the clutches of contaminated ecclesiology,
Doomed to be denominationally dead until all hope is gone.
Ask not to build, expand or plant a church with me
For I cannot escape that in which I am set.

I alone stand doctrinally sound, to the degree
That heresy shall never be deemed to have disabled me.
And for your radical thoughts, they just frighten me.
Wretched man that I am, who shall deliver me from my
   conceit?

Once I was told that, over me, a glass ceiling had been placed.
Tradition was its name and, having been polished by the past,
Nothing was visible to me as I looked up,
Though those looking down could see my plight of paralysis.

They pitied me, knowing there never was invented
The means to smash the shinning surface from the underside.
Looking out, I could see nothing for all refracted light
Reflected myself to me. How happy am I in that!

Contained within the confines of my colourful cocoon
I can live life with a contentment you cannot comprehend,
Let alone live and share. Your loss is my diminution,
destruction and decay.
I am blind to all but me and mine; it has thus been and will
   forever be.

'Wretched man that I am, who shall deliver me from my self-contentment?'
Wherein lies adventure, growth, and the future God has planned?
With no escape are the possibilities only to be found in what has been?
But who is a hero who wants only what has forever been?

Where is one who has courageous insight?
Confidence to trust that which has never been trusted?
Courage to contemplate another truth? To discover word and attitude
That will destroy the cell, the cage, the sphere and ceiling made of glass.

Bringing liberty with its future, its potential and its growth.
'O glory of the lighted mind.'
'How dead I've been, how dumb, how blind.'
To quote Saul Kane of Masefield's, 'Everlasting Mercy'.

The Christ creation is nothing less than all things new.
He who escapes that way is birthed in freedom.
Only He can save the wretched man that I am.
Bringing life in all its fullness. Liberation in eternity.

4. Theoretical Theory

Tools of trade for management, by compulsive acquisition
    gleaned,
The Bell Curve, Risk, and Critical Path analysis
With SWOT and PEST or PESTLE. Even SLEPT!
Words we use to define the thinking of this art.

What is being analysed and what is being weighed?
To whom is account to be given and will due notice be taken?
A whole industry spawned upon what men have done,
Or intended 'might' be done, until the cry of caution rings.

A parasitical profession for good or ill, as a tree might stand
    or fall.
But what is this that has grown and grown
Faster than entrepreneurs can breed?
Someone has to do something before the analyst can analyse.

In the beginning, what? By whom?
Did fear of future dissection deter the pioneer?
Where, today, stand those giants of invention
Who braved to break the mould and did all things new?

Past performance is no guarantee of what will be, so we are
    told
Though encouraged to believe the opposite.
'To dare to do' has lost its soul in the mists of 'what might be'.
Has the time come round again that all must dare to do?

Can a call be heard that this is the day to dare to be?
Does vision lead the task and call the inquisitorial

To lag behind not lead the way?
When what is done that has not been done before, curtails not

Contemplation that releases celebration, can a way ahead be seen?
There walk the pioneers who leave perfection for those who rush to follow.
So the new question gains in status:
'Ask not, how it can be improved. Ask what is there to be accomplished.'

5. Church

Was there ever a word more maligned, mistrusted,
 misunderstood?
Standing for a hundred things and none.
A word that strives to contain the greatest concept corralling
 man,
Yet used, misused and magnified. Distorting truth,
To the deceiver's delight: blinding us, befuddling us,
Leaving us limp, uncertain and confused.

From Latin descent, we moved down the definition road
Of 'buildings' rather than 'a gathering'.
Time has taught us to forget truth enshrouded in the mists of
 ancient past.
Let tradition stand co-equal with all truth,
Too late to change time-honoured thinking of the 'saints'.
What is will be until 'another generation cometh'.

Jerusalem, Rome, Alexandria and Constantinople in early
 centuries,
Though not necessarily in that chronological succession,
Headed East and West in 'orthodoxy'; giving us the first
 divisions.
Who could have dreamt such small numbers would explode?
Akin to the 'Big Bang' sending thirty-four thousand
 denominations
Spiralling into an expanding space. Often each is called a
 church.

Then other epithets accrue, as theologians contemplate the
 incomprehensible.

The Church Universal is one such. Holy, Catholic, and Apostolic
Pertain to a different time, having Nicene as a geographical locale
And, to set it in time, a date of 325 AD: the first Ecumenical Council.
Militant and Triumphant both belong in the description, as do Visible and Invisible.
Gathering the living and the dead, all to be counted in its number.

Might now be the time to return to roots?
To declare the first intent of word and deed? To ask, again, Ekklesia's truth.
'Called out', as I remember. A group, assemblage, or maybe congregation.
Certainly a gathering of people.
So how can you go to Church if you already 'are' the church?
Conundrums capable of confining thought and leaving confusion.

Lest any think the serious intent of theological verse
Will pass by the author's own judgement, let me destroy that myth,
Roundly declaring my conclusion.
The Church: no more, no less, than the 'Congregation of the King'.

6. Science and Religion

I poured some liquids in a glass
And stirred the mix for integration.
Deceptive though appearance is,
The end result was separation.

The oil in tiny droplets formed,
Suggesting frequent agitation might,
In spite of all the contrary 'truth',
Lead to a more mature mix.

Standing there it caught my eye,
Having turned away a while.
Two liquids in one container, balanced
In equilibrium, one above the other.

Introduce an emulsifier and all things change.
Oil is no longer oil and
Water no longer water.
With what are you left? A gooey sludge.

Google might provide its name.
To me, however, there is no recall.
Of far greater worry and concern is the
Question, can the un-mixable be un-mixed?

What, in another experiment,
If the ingredients were changed?
Replace the liquids with contentious
Quest of Science and Religion?

Time was when, of the two, ascendency
Gave pride of place to religion:
Science, its servant and handmaid.
Dispute brought often painful death.

Brave scientists could not be gagged
Succumbing to no threat of fire,
Still to observe, count, calculate,
Express, and fear no cruel consequence.

At first, they played the game,
Seeing themselves of the same mix,
One. No separation in their minds,
Only integration, but never at any cost.

Yet, well before 'religion' raised its intolerant head,
Pythagoras, Democritus, and one Aristarchus
Of original bent of mind, pursued
Great thoughts of universal scale and consequence.

Succeeding in a the proud succession
Came Epicures, Anaximander and Heraclitus,
Only to be followed by the like of Galileo,
Copernicus, Kepler, Newton and, of late, Hawking.

A backward glance, for I had looked away again,
Found attention drawn towards the glass.
Just as before, having only one fact in common
Both being liquid, one boldly stood upon the other.

No integration, only separation. The postulate,
Of course, is God. 'Progenitor extraordinaire',

In creative mode: calling not one but countless
Universes to be, as boiling pan releases bubbles.

To look for your science in religion,
Or, as some do, your religion in your science,
Could be said to be trying, yet again,
To un-mix the un-mixable. And visa versa so to speak?

But is that not to, yet again, confuse the two?
Science and Religion? Which now stands as
One upon another? Renaissance, notwithstanding,
Has God become the first Great Divine Emulsifier?

Is Man, creation's crown (late of Greek
Thinking - body, mind and spirit- but of Hebrew
An integrated whole) the unnamed gooey sludge
Consequent upon divine emulsification?

'No separation,' says the theologian,
'Of any constituent part of flesh and spirit,
Save at the time of death, when comes
The great divide leading on to Judgement.'

'Not so,' contends the scientist, 'for you
Cannot prove, hold, analyse, and dissect,
By constant repetition of your peers,
Existence of nonphysical.'

In death united, a conversation
Might be heard as theologian says to scientist,
'Are you sure that I'm not here?' And scientist to theologian says,

'As sure as I am not, you are.' And versa visa, so to speak.

7. Grace

He said it was a series and I expected much.
And 'much' would be the word as week unfolded, week on week,
Introducing all facets and features, through familiar faces.
'Twas upended, dissected, described and tweaked.

First, inspiration from congregation came,
Suggesting foundational concept: caught, taught, or copied,
In groups of three to four, and blended until,
In glorious isolation standing, its truth appeared.

Where majority shop, I know not, but the same adage applies.
If it looks too good to be true, rest assured truth will out.
So when the cry was heard 'it's free', there had to be some doubt,
For truth, contrary to accumulated experience, leaves uncertainty.

Quite clearly, there was work to do and it had to be done,
To convince the congregation of pillars, upon which it thought it rested,
Were not in the least bit untenable; when in face of prevailing insight,
What is free is so free, even freer, that for debtor the debt has been paid.

Consternation was written on faces, which once knew their 'knower' knew.
Now, however, being told free is free and 'grace' is the only contender,

New hope could emerge; forged in furnace of life, declaring accused
Go free at expense of the One that went that way, by a route called Calvary.

What once moulded and fashioned my life, with its ins and outs,
Laid aside on an altar with a label called 'self,' could in smoke be seen rising,
Dispersed in the mists of the morning as warmth began its work.
Now giving birth to new patterns of living, consequential on
Calvary's cost.

Told over and over my relationships mattered, forever, as always.
Was I right? Try as I tried, I could not get it right putting 'self' in
Pole place, expectant of others to submit to my case.
Before me now stood the one who would lead, letting me follow Calvary's need.

My life now determined by a pattern of 'truth,' my destiny asked
Not for long-lasting proof, but simply if space could be found where my
End be assured, being freed from the shackles of cold, clammy death,
As was given the thief staked by the side of a man crowned
Calvary's King.

A weight weighed me down, which in church they call Sin,

With no diminution, day upon day, neither in month nor on year, try as I may
Till one day, the mirror of pain I had caused showed me so clearly
The need to be free. Looking up, there it was. On Calvary's Tree.

All defences disarmed and nowhere to turn, my strength seemed to wilt
At the thought of all that was needed to accomplish the end.
Having badgered my will and exhausted my thoughts, with no resolution
Left to back up the fight, He took all on himself: had it nailed to a tree.

To look at the tree brought me up with a start, as I saw what was there,
Suspended in part, by those nails driven in flesh, with no thought for the pain, holding
Man and my burdens, and your burdens too, cemented by love for no price we could pay.
A Cross, a man, and the mountains of sin, on a far distant hill known forever. Amen.

It is said my heart melted, for clearly I knew He got my 'deserts'.
To grave they would go, with him, to be buried below.
Death was the Captor his destiny set,
But mine the delight of an endless release from the
Strength of what's dead, to the power of what lives, from the tomb 'neath the cross.

Then money was mentioned and its correlation with grace.
Could words be changed and the unquantifiable quantified?
Certainly, in the pleading of a Paul, it looks as though the Macedons outdid all.
Not from income, abundance, but poverty and grace.
Exemplary grace.

Ah, we haven't finished yet. Maybe the best is kept to the last.
It seems generosity, for all it's worth, has nought to do with money and cash,
But rather all to do with grace: grace upon grace and then more grace.
As Paul again contends, 'the all-surpassing grace of God, given you.'

'In conclusion', came today and all seemed low key until the truth
Was 'outed' from Acts Thirteen: forty-three. Something to be continued in,
Walked in, lived in, rejoiced in. An inescapable act of God for each and all;
The birthright of believers; bought and paid for with toil, suffering and blood.

To buy it, don't even try; for the price has been paid. Even now, you have nothing
Save what he will give, out of generous love and his freedom of will,
Released by the Father. Inexorable power to live in these days; the Spirit's
Compulsion, embedded in us, to live now the grace that is seen on the Cross.

Finale.

'The grace of God has appeared offering salvation to all.

Teaching us to say 'no' to all ungodly ways and all worldly passion.

Living upright lives, letting God control all passion and self in this present age.

Whilst we wait the appearing of the Saviour Son, who gave himself

Freely to redeem us and purify for himself, a people his own, to do only good.'

(Titus 2:11-13)

8. Poetry and Prophecy

They share three syllables.
Least, at my last count.
But should you encounter
My mathematics of late,
Such slender calculation
Cannot bear any weight.

Other things in common
May yet be seen to hold,
As when, the other day
A snippet of but three
Words fell, full-frontal,
In my brain with nothing
There to follow on.

Only when to paper I
Put pen, or rather weary
Fingers to the keyboard
Found their way,
Did any thought, or plan,
Or idea, propel the brain
Cells further forward,
To give form to ovule.

In the moment I
Remembered situation
Of great similitude,
Three words were there.
Alone they stood
On the threshold

Of my mind. She too,
Anticipation rapt,
Stood still before me.

Only as I spoke
Those words did others
Follow on. Her
Expectation was rewarded.
And tears began
To roll down cheeks
That seemed so ill
Prepared, as mascara
Ran and was misplaced,
And sniffles stirred.

So Prophecy and Poetry
Do have things in common,
Beside three syllables.
There, in the unknown future,
Unwritten or unspoken,
Hanging in the balance
Until bold beginning,
Speech or written
Word remains unborn.
Then, perchance, a flow
Begins a spring.

9. Is It Just Me?

One thing has always troubled me. 'Only one?'
I hear you asking as knowing me better than myself
Releases in your understanding a comprehension
I could never match, even if a mirror was brought into play.

It has to do with music and time dimension too.
Words can be understood and, where it becomes
Necessity, can be acted upon. 'Halt! Who goes there?'
A friend or foe could well outcome determine.

Music is a sound sequence as much as any word.
But where is comprehension that could command
A battalion of soldiers in serried ranks to 'shun',
Or an 'if you please', unlock the proffered path?

It is a sound that can be called a 'note' and, in
Succession joined, be called a 'tune'. In harmony
Pleasant to the ear, in chord or discord joined.
Symphony, concerto, for quintet or quartet formed.

But what are you left holding in your mind?
I am perplexed for, without being unkind, you have
Only been listening to a noise that has to compete
In a noisy world, where silence is a joyful sound.

Middle C began the flow, which ended with a 'flat'
Of some kind, that memory has dislodged from
The wearisome recesses of an aged mind bent on
 Retention of other more important issues of the day!

The speech was moving and demanded a response.
The tirade lasted hour on hour. Only he who spoke was
    moved.
The instructions could just as well be read.
Whilst the proclamation was so well received, everyone
    agreed.

But leaving the concert, just what was mine
For all the money paid? I watched such skilful
Fingers work in harmony with breath, but now,
What now have I to do, or where to go, to follow you?

And where does that time-dimension come into play?
At any given point in time, it is only one or maybe few
Notes that I can hear. Take the 'before' and 'after'
From your mind, with what are you then left?

Sounds which form words, with them I can contend.
But sounds in succession, gathered without a word,
Seem worse than in some far-off land where
Even words not understood still form some other tongue.

It troubles me now, as it has always done.
But confession is at hand and words have to be used.
I could live my life without the words and be forever deaf.
Yet to live without my music would be a living death.
Nothing is as powerful or profound, eliciting
Emotions nothing else can ever do. Never have I
Experienced power in such dimensions as Paganini's
Variations on a theme from Rossini's Moses.

It has a task for me. Repentance, it is called.

To hold back tears and not confess; to stop and
Turn around and, in the Maker's path, set reluctant feet in
New found ways of increasing obedience.

Still trying to define the indefinable, I listen
In rapt attention to those notes that had duly
Been assembled in the most amazing patterns: if
They were but light, would the world completely dazzle.

Music has a way to unlock and do what words cannot.
When words are clothed with music, a journey is begun.
However, that can only take us where the confines
Of the syllables allow. Some new experience is waiting.

The journey of the sound alone allows the soul to soar
For beyond the limits of the mind weighed down
With argument, with wit, wisdom and philosophy:
Couching in confusion ideas, thoughts and more.
But we are left with only words to describe the
Journey of the soul, when all the time the need is there
To be set free. Could there ever come a day when such
Reality might be released? Might that day be death?

Was there a rumour, long ago, that sounds were heard
In Heaven? And was that rumour rectified as, for a space
Of half an hour, silence was said to reign? Or have I been
Reading again that book that only ill-advised are wont to
    open?

Thinking of departure then from this wearisome existence,
I can imagine words, and yet more words, echoing
Around some lofty space that would be far better

Filled with intertwining harmony and music sound.

When that day comes, as someday it most surely must,
It would be pure delight aloft to be borne on some
Soaring soprano sounds that might, just might,
Ascend to heights, then with the angels blend.

10. Does Nothing Change?

What, I wondered, before the bugle sounded the call,
Rallied the troops to battle stations and the charge?
Could it have been the loudest voice, whose echo
Was picked up by other voices loud and passed
Back and forth along the lines drawn up for some
Supposed noble conflict between tribe and tribe?

My first teacher, taking those of nine and ten towards
The test of something later found to be 'Eleven Plus', used
Ruler on our knuckles to aid our concentration in the
Classroom.
Then on Sundays, cherubic like, sang alto in the choir.
Yet one thing she said stays with me to this day.
'Necessity is the mother of invention, forget it not.'

A stick and stone might break my bone. Maybe thus it started.
In later years the call came in a brown, sealed, paper
   envelope
Emblazoned with the royal command, 'On His Majesty's
   Service.'
So summoned to the ranks I went, with not a little fear.
From sticks and stones, lances and arrows sharp of necessity,
Had spawned invention of such great sophistication: Atomic
Weaponry.

Those of High Command had chain communication through
   all ranks.
No loudest call, no bugle sound, rather a silent, coded,
   electronic buzz
Could set a world at war: not tribe against tribe, but nations

against nations.
That is, of course, till every enrolled recruit, not exempt
From the general populace, possesses other electronic devices
At whose invitations every citizen can fill the streets.

First the Police, but soon they are overrun. Then the Army, firing death,
Soon has to ask 'how many of our own?' The power from Premier to people
Creates confusion, as it should, for the day has dawned when those
Whose voices only could say 'Yes', now by the million can say 'No',
As blurred fingers frantically engage the keypads of each new gizmo.
'Let those who have eyes see, and those who have ears hear.'

11. Voice for the Voiceless

When all is said and done, almost all can speak.
But, is it not the hearing, and who hears, that matters most?
The cry can be from far away or nearer than you think,
What of the hearing though, where no noise makes a sound?
What of the voice that mouths the words your language
Cannot cope? The silent cry heard only in the heart.
The loudest shout in empty desert wastes.
The tears that tell the silent story and asks the age old
　question,
Where were you? Excuses crowd, like vultures round a
　corpse,
Ready to disturb the gathered scavengers of endless plain.
All far too busy to cock an ear or turn a head toward the
Distant articulation of another's plight. Here there is
Something not to be missed, so eyes down, ears shut,
My life's my own and it will stay that way, unless
Advantage is to me to change my course and use that
Vile phrase, 'self interest'. Who invented such an absurdity
Encouraging me to do some good for you when I will benefit?

I want to help! The world's too big; its problems are immense.
There was a day when I thought I heard the faintest cry.
Something in me stirred an exploration, but I am only one.
Uncertain still if I had really heard what others could ignore,
Or had there been a sound, like the wardrobes speak at
Night, of nothing consequential, stirring only a passing fear
That does not necessitate the switching of the light.
Yet it was real, distinct, full of clarity, vibrating in my soul.
Now I'm uncomfortable and unable to articulate what
Moves me to say, 'I will be a voice for the voiceless,

Let me go.' You ask me where, I cannot tell you. All
Because what I heard I only thought I heard and now, for
Confirmation, look. There you cannot help, for I must hear
The cry again. Now I am lost, for where was I when first that
Sound disturbed my inner self? Recalling not location clear,
I look to repeat that inner disposition that unlocked in me a
Hearing, not of ears, but of the heart; commanding
    obedience.

I look to you, but who are you to tell me where all this is
    going now?
I know it's going to cost, not cash, though well it might, but
    then it might
Mean me! Uncertainty plagues the soul until the moment of
Surrender. Raising of a flag of white, the lifting high of hands,
The laying down of all construed offence, abandonment to
    other;
All ways of giving expression to obsequious grovelling in the
    dust.
Total capitulation of the will is what is freely given, as slave to
    master,
Soldier to commander, and convert to Christ the King.
The surge within still lingers on, finding paralysis of thought
    and limb.
What can I do, where can I go, which way to turn, will you
    come too?
The days are short, the years rush by, as forever destiny
    beckons
Ever more strongly and the cries increase in volume as in
    number.
The day has come, the time is near, distractions all
    abandoned.

If it is to be, and it most surely must, then decision day
Has come. Beyond the far horizon lies the goal and getting there
Has urgency. Brain, limbs, and likelihood must bend and yield.
Today's the day that I become a 'Voice for the Voiceless.'

(Dedicated to Margaret Nyumbu)

12. Alone in the City

Alone in the city I stood.
It all looked so familiar.
On which continent was I?
In which great continental capital?

It seemed as though I knew
All, yet no one knew of me.
Fashion, far from local,
Displayed its universality.

From what nations do we come?
Our languages divide so ignorance,
The breeder of all fear,
Abounds and cowers and binds.

Meaningful relationships,
Impossible to forge, find
Expression only in grunts and groans,
Never names disclosing.

Pain is felt but to whom to turn
Is a question often asked?
Bright lights bedazzle but
It is the darkness that conceals.

Both light and dark have
The capacity to hide the one
Who knows no one and about whom
No one cares or casts a glance.

What isolation inflicts upon the soul
Is not the pain a doctor or a nurse address
In A & E of city life. It's a sanitised
Supermarket where the credit-card is king.

I have no credit or the cash
To keep alongside spenders.
Holding the same is likened to
Grasping dry sand as it returns to ground.

Where bus and coach and even train
Can be refuges of warmth, true
Aloneness is a chill no heat can comprehend,
Freezing the marrow of bone and brain.

Walls are blank. No
Pictures hung to hide
Imperfections of the plaster
Or cracks and condensation.

Stairs to climb. Deprived
Of breath because of numbers.
And arrival did not lend
Enchantment to the view.

Why do you look at me like that?
Your gaze goes on beyond,
As though I am not there.
I think you do not see me.

Experiencing aloneness in a crowd
Is not that unfamiliar.

At football match or cinema
No one would complain.

Wherever born and bred within
The city of your birth
Tells a different story of confusion,
Lack of self-belief and inner grief.

When Woodbine Willy of Great War
Fame, spoke of Jesus in the City,
He spoke no truer word than this, 'When Jesus
Came to Birmingham, they simply passed him by.'

For Lima Pike.

13. Why is it Monday When it Feels Like Friday?

Astonishment! Surprise! Amazement swept across his face.
Suddenly he exclaimed, 'Why is it Monday when it feels like Friday?'
The flickering thought was gone before it came to rest, save for one.

He was with friends. All who were present wanted to be there,
Wanted to support him, respond to his invitation for help.
No 'must'. No 'ought'. No 'should'. Compulsion was not a constituent.

He was doing what he loved; exposing his thoughts for the critical
Consideration of others, irrespective of age, ambition, accreditation
Or aspiration. Close to his heart, the intent to move all further on.

He was excited by the theme: rooted in his heart, expressive of his
Relationship, of highest priority in life and love. Worship: no longer
A warm-up for the Word; a prelude for a preacher; but 'stand alone'.

God's gift to his creation when He breathed in Man His life. The means,
He said, to motivate the reciprocal response. To return the true affection
Of heart to heart. Creator and created, bound as one

together. Perfection.

So busy were his days that Friday saw the opportunity for sanity
And social interaction, where excitement had potential to peak.
So, though it was a Monday, inside it felt like Friday. Sheer delight.

For Nick.

14. Compassion

It is not a feeling, it has to be an action,
Argued the young enthusiast.
Compassion.

Then again, the eyes can speak and the
Glance she gave said it all.
Compassion.

A turn towards, rather than a turn away,
Stirred deep hope.
Compassion.

There was something about the touch:
It was so warm.
Compassion.

No one else spoke and the silence was
So cruel, until he said 'Yes'.
Compassion.

There was no knowledge of a name, only
A strong embrace.
Compassion.

Alone he stood in the corner of the playground.
Unnoticed, until she approached.
Compassion.

Tears neither rose nor flowed; they tumbled.
An outstretched hand caught one.

Compassion.

Everything was gone, destroyed, erased.
The blanket's embrace was warm.
Compassion.

Cold and damp, she huddled in the doorway.
The warm soup, sufficient.
Compassion.

15. Where Fell the Thirty Pieces?

The hands had sheen, from regular handling of coins.
But these thirty pieces were not ordinary.
Silver for sure, and of intrinsic value,
They seemed so hot, with intention dark.

Red, with much spilt blood to come,
They could not be held for long and destiny
Decreed they would, and should, be thrown
Across religion's face, on Temple floor.

Where fell those thirty pieces? Rolling through
The temples of the years, declaring sacred
Satisfaction; a job that needed to be done which
Someone ought, and must, and should so rightly do.

Stained by slaughter, slavery, bigotry, bias,
Racism, violence, abuse of every kind,
Discrimination, deceit, forced labour and migration,
Victimisation vindicated by fatuous argument of every kind.

The tragedy, not of one season in one century far removed,
But by repetition upon repetition, and in the name
Of every faith and none, in flames of conflict for
Control. 'I'm right, you're wrong. It's mine, not yours.'

Thirty pieces rolling still, now stained with oil and mineral
Wealth: now stained with forests disappeared,
Vast tracts of uninhabitable land; poisoned by the greed
Of one, all at another's expense: both man and beast.

Betrayal was cheap for only thirty pieces. Cheaper
Still, in the temples of today, where greed still rules
And nations crush nations, all for nought; count
Debt not by millions, nor by billions, but in trillions.

It bought a man his death, from which some have learned
Still to war, destroy, kill and trash it as no consequence,
Or use, as pretence, to stand against a foe of their own
    making.
Who picked them up? Maybe there is one amongst my
    change.

16. Majesty

I saw a man in majesty. It could have been the one
Inspiration used, by Elgar, for 'Pomp and Circumstance.'
His flowing robes swept to his feet and even past,
So appearance of gliding was the illusion, or at least
On tiptoe, holding fast to a strong staff with gold
And jewels encrusted. There, upon his head, giving
Semblance of outrageous height, strengthened material
Of colours royal. He had an entourage all clothed in white,
With crimson caps and belted waists of considerable girth
Confined. He alone made gestures broad and wide, before the
Bowing heads and outstretched arms holding aloft
What looked like flowers, cheering as he passed them by.
Inquiry was now foremost. Who could this be? Resplendent
In such opulence, displaying ostentatiously such sumptuous
Attire. Listening carefully, I was told no ownership could
Be involved, for he was representative, no more, no less.
He was proxy for another. But for whom? I asked myself.

I saw a man in majesty. Unclothed from head to toe. A
Bleeding back, a bleeding front, that left a bright red flow.
Supporting, yet to be 'support', a cross-framed wooden
Shape. It gave exaggerated height, robbed of nobility
By the bending back weighed down with bruise and pain.
A stumble, followed by the whip's lash that scored the back
Again, drove the tortured form onward up the hill, which
    very
Shape, they said, resembled the hollow skull his head was
Destined to become when death and birds had had their fill.
Summit attained; the wood thrown down; the body nailed
In place; and all was raised by muscled soldiers' strength

Until, with a resounding thud of flesh-tearing force, it
Settled in its pre-dug socket, standing aloft and bearing
In majesty a man for cloak, crimson blood, and dust.
Inquiry was now foremost. Who could this be? Resplendent
In a death few human eyes could countenance, coloured
From the pallet of humanity's flesh, dragged through the dirt.
His entourage, a jeering mob and soldiers standing bright.
He too, a representative. No more, no less, and I believe
As I am told, that that might well be me and all mankind.
He was my proxy, attaining for me what I was helpless to attain.
From His death, He gave me life. Can I, should I, ought I,
To compare the two? My quandary and I am set to wondering
If it also might be yours?

17. Just a Thought

There is but one thing among many,
From days spent in Africa,
That has claimed my attention
From time to time. Why is it so easy
To spot the pastor and the politician?
Because they alone, are the overweight.

18. Gratitude

What is it about gratitude that wields
Such power to stir emotions deep?
Two simple words: 'thank you.'

They stand alone, or maybe accompanied
By simple gestures of the hands and
Arms, a shake, a hug or, maybe, an embrace.

Sometimes even a gift is given, of
No great meaningful significance, save
Ability to bind up the broken heart.

A sad reflection that in such a painful
World, we find it hard to give expression
To, perhaps, the most powerful of evocations.

19. Laments Can't Hide Truth

A Bible book called Lamentations.
And yet another overflows with
Laments, by name of Psalms known.
We are asked where laments
Feature in our faith, finding
Expression in worship offered.

Illumination comes our way
When understanding gives a chance.
The word to link with a lament
Has surely to be Truth. Is my lament
That laments are scarce; evidence
Of truth lacking in what is offered?

My only answer is affirmative.
I share an equal guilt that truth is
Often a scarce commodity in that
Called worship, arising from my lips,
Be it Saturday or Sunday or any other
Day or night when I cry out.

To introduce lament is to confront
The truth, or maybe an even greater
Degree of it than I'm prepared to disclose.
An aching heart is skilled in its reply.
'Yes, I'm fine,' the crowning lie,
Enabling my escape from your probing.

20. Heart to Heart

Did I know or understand what I meant, that day
I whispered I love you?
Life has elapsed and still the truth's unclear.

Now is my time to talk with you,
To walk with you,
To find your eyes to hold my gaze.

It's been so long and I've missed you.
Have you missed me?
Not found the focus through the tears?

It's true: you search and search again.
To give up is alien to you.
For me, to wander off is in my soul.

Oh! Were it not so: that I could sit and stay,
To linger here
For hour on hour, and still then have no certainty.

Wrapped in your arms, security I knew.
When did it evaporate,
That, now, the missing strong embrace evades me?

Your love, its grip cannot loosen or detach.
So what is it that I miss?
The warmth, the touch, the gentle embrace?

It is to return that haunts me deep within.
The dream is real.

The entwining is horizontal but so secure.

Every night, as my eyes begin to close,
You are there beside me.
Ecstasy cannot describe the sensations that pulsate.

The call to love contains an emptiness belying
Truth it should contain.
What is the reality that all accept but so few know?

An everlasting presence: from whom escape is impossibility.
To laugh, to cry, to share,
An everlasting ejaculation of every sensual experience

Where two are one, and one are two, and procreation
An unheard indulgence;
Lost in selfless wonder of a world where there is only love.

Is that death described as Life Eternal?
An exit being entrance;
Where earthbound flies, death awakes, and Love wins.

21. The White Wolves of Eastcote Grange

The story goes that, as the age of ice receded,
The all-pervading colour white dazzled the perspective
And all left-living creatures cast their coats for white.
'Twas later said that fearful howls were all that
Could be heard in Arden's forested tracks.
Today, a memory of the frozen scene was stirred.

The White Wolves of Eastcote Grange,
With contemptuous gesticulation, lift their heads
And open wide their mouths.
Blood-curdling howls that freeze the frame
Are never heard, for silence rules.
The mouths quietly close as heads droop down.
Their ferocious posture is again resumed.

Three there are in adulthood and three in
Newborn state. One male and two females seems
A fair assessment but, for the offspring, who
Could tell, as parental proximity prevents
Closer inspection. Yet something seems a
Little out of place and, though all the wasteland
Is white, unlikely cohabiters attend.

White-clad trees surround the mountain's
Snow-shrouded height, where proudly stands
The stag, head held aloft, bearing his many pointed
Antlers, all strangely white as well. Whilst
Below, not one belying the scenic shade of white,
Stand grouped both polar bears and penguins,
Each proudly portraying their offspring too.

Sadly, the scene is staged and all livestock
Move mechanically, securely stored through
Spring and Summer in cosseted containers, ready to
Make their annual appearance at the Garden
Centre's Christmas display. Anomalies disturb not
The child's imagination, which sees here nothing
Of which to be afraid, nought to ignite a nightmare.

But the delight it gives to young and old
Cannot be denied, as all are seen to pause and,
With admiration, talk of the loving skill that,
Yet again, this year has brought forth pleasure
In the careful construction, lovingly contrived:
To display the unreality in the magic of this scene,
That holds attention whilst some, at least, may buy.

22. Change and Changeability

All my life, if truth be told,
One thing has dominated:
And that the will, desire, determination
To change another's ways.

So set before the listening ear
Such truth, such unchanging truth
That, apprehended by its clarity,
The heart and life would turn.

But now I have discovered
There is only one that I can change,
And that is me; my life for moulding
To the truth I have so long sought to portray.

23. Confidentiality

The Union seemed by compassion overcome.
Appointed from the Floor, selected by his mates,
A representative, duly elected, took his place
On the committee.

Its purpose: worker's welfare, first and foremost,
They were told. Where help might be afforded
All would pull together, ease his plight, giving support
Through the committee.

Returning to his workplace after hearing the first
Case, a plight had touched him deeply.
Compassion stirred from deep within,
Not only by committee.

Approaching now his work mates, oblivious
To all sense of feeling, he walked along and
Blurted out his comment 'What's think of 'e then?'
No longer on committee.

24. Silence in Sounds

Desert fathers, seeking silence and seclusion,
Almost inadvertently invented monasticism,
Which has survived nearly two thousand years.

Confronted with sights and sounds of our 'today',
Does the desert still hold its magnetism, pulling
Our emotive souls to seek aloneness and solitude?

For some of course, but what for those who cannot
Escape the Number Eleven, and its perambulations
Of the Inner Circle, in the noisy brashness of Birmingham?

What is there that those fathers found, that we
Cannot find upon the upper deck? Spiritual wisdom,
Insight, or integration with eternity whilst drawing breath?

There is a belief that I hold dear and it is this:
That God, through a multiplicity of ways, is not
Handicapped in His communication skills.

I need to hear, I need to know, and He knows that I do.
What will he move to circumnavigate my deafness
To all things of his Spirit because my ears can't hear?

Recollection tells me of one who heard the Father's
Voice in solitude, silence and the hubbub of the market place;
Who, at the climax of a cross, had intimacy complete.

That too, he shared as all his short life he had done.
That too, he shares in each contemporary moment whether

I am hushed to silence or cannot hear to think.

Some of course were born for that. But when you have
Your place and know it is ordained for you, then his
Communion with your soul fulfils the hearing of your heart.

25. Gathering Water Melons

Long was the road but straight.
Unusual for this Lebanese landscape.
Traffic was light, the highway wide.
Before us, a lorry heavy laden
With the largest, greenest water melons.
Our transport, a small sixteen-seater coach,
Had seen many a better day.
Slowly the distance between us reduced.
Soon, speed synchronised, no attempt was
Made to overtake, for driver and guide had made a plan.
Full of concentration, our guide hung from the door,
His hands entangled in the other's load and
Soon a plump ripe melon was being passed
Among the passengers. 'How many?' he called.
There was no greed and six sufficed, as we
Passed on, completing the complex overtake.

26. The Ballad of Bay Four

Sentinel-like they stand, awaiting their companions.
The thirty minute cleaning cycle has elapsed.
Plastic pipes, recumbent in their place, connected to life-saving
Artificial kidneys whose membranes separate the 'waste'.

Coupling with companions for the four-hour stint
Is by way of needles, sharp or blunt, inserted with
Differing degrees of skill, as those trained in this
Form of torture move among those condemned to Dialysis.

Bay Four, I'm sure, is not unique, though sometimes I wonder.
Who gives it special quality are, of course, its recipients.
Queuing in the light and dark, dependent on the season,
Rain or snow, mist or fog, and sometimes sunshine.

Soon after six-fifteen assembly begins, as those arriving
In their cars foregather, with their bags and blankets.
Up the slope, they make their way, hoping the yellow cone's
In place that bids them welcome, whilst holding the door ajar.

First to weigh, to see what damage last night drinks have done.
Then to the chair repair, and make all necessary adjustments
Prior to climbing aboard the beast, to start the four-hour ride.
But first a surreptitious look around to see whose duty fell today.

Blood pressure, taken twice, once before, once after.

Then it's written down. The pack is torn apart, sterile all
That is inside. The tapes are readied, one, two, three, four
And maybe five or six. After a while, you get to know each
    nurse's number.

Details are fed into the machine, almost like mortician's notes.
Date of birth, height, weight (not width, nor what you did the
    night before).
Some things are whispered, as the soul is bared for this saucy
Sentinel who, with his signature of confidentiality, nothing
    will disclose.

Then time for the connections to be made, with varying
    degrees
Of pain, dependent on so many different factors. Is mood
    one?
The pump speed set, all details logged, the folder filled and
Innohep applied to the machine that does not flinch at the
    insertion.

Then comes the time, with unerring frequency, of 'monthly
    bloods'
Which are are never known to lie. The extricated samples, to
    the lab
Dispatched, give readings that disclose both 'what' you ate
    and drank,
Not 'where'. Upon these forensic findings, your fate is fixed.

Time now to turn the monster around so that buttons can be
    pressed
Extinguishing the warning lights, when troublesome they get.
Here the greatest care is taken for, in the top left corner, is the

switch
That turns the whole thing off; and woe betides the perpetrator.

This electric chair, in which each is confined to complete the sentence,
Adjusts in every way conceivable, and then some, if you look beneath
To view the warning sign that reads, 'do not touch into the mechanic'.
Headsets on, adjust for volume and station, but don't ring the nurse.

It's time to settle down now and the banter to begin, peculiar to the bay.
Football's course is short, with cricket only just ahead. But what outstrips
The rest by far is the television's stock-in-trade, the plethora of Soaps.
Sometimes, some news may be picked up: like the passing of one named Max.

Shops can feature too, as when Bon Marche went bust and vouchers
Lost their value. First, it is the faintest scent, increasing as the toast
Gets near, closely followed by the tea. Here introduced as well, can
Be another nurse or yet the ubiquitous Health Care Assistant.

A new dimension of conversation now begins, usually carrying mirth,

Save when news of someone's demise is being passed around.
New shoes or coat; nets and traffic noise; the wife too,
Not here to defend herself, has her last exploit revealed.

All in some way helps to pass the time that drags on interminably.
Sometimes the eyes begin to close and mouths begin to open
As sleep, that blissful but elusive state, announces its presence with a snore.
Then again, it's not that which awakes, but the whistler's higher pitch.

The first sign that the trial is coming to an end is the rattling of the
Roller, as the apron is released; then the fight begins to get it round the neck,
Smooth it down the front, and tie it at the back in one deft motion.
Wash back complete, needles removed, it's time to stem the flow.

When the waiting is over and the weight is checked again,
The all-clear can be given, signalling the start of another wait,
Should your situation be that you are brought by ambulance
And by ambulance return. For others, engines start and barrier lifts.

Every other weekday, this palaver is pursued to keep alive the victims
Of failed kidneys. This is their life support and however far away
They go each has to return, enduring yet more hours of

cleansing blood.
Brave souls who sometimes wait to hear the phone: 'We have
a kidney.'

(Dedicated to my wife, Jennifer, who for eight long years
endured this ordeal)

27. To Think Outside the Box

In my dream, I thought I saw the universe.
Yet my eyes seemed open, causing confusion,
Followed on by yet more uncertainty.
The sky was endless blue, allowing only clouds to define
 distance.
The night was black, of equatorial African dimension.
Delineating the darkness were the stars, two planets,
A moon and an array of geostationary orbiters.
Yet in abundance, vast abundance, far outweighing all
Of day or night to be seen, were the oceans of space.
Some questions forged themselves deep in my mind.
Concept of space as emptiness, nothingness.
What is there, is not, or space ceases to be.
So what divides what's there, holding it apart?
What is encountered after the exit from our atmosphere?
Through what do space-exploring craft pass when
Traveling light-years there, but never back?

Hubble illuminates what's there but can it see what's, not?
Man maps our planetary system putting it in space,
Calling it a solar system, set within a galaxy.
Then, multiplying millions, creates the word called
Universe, which seems to comprise more nothingness
Than substance. Where am I going inside my head?
Now there's a thought, for do not particles have
Orbits in the atoms, I am told, that make me up?
So in their register of tininess, are they too held
In the abundance of emptiness I might call space?
Is then this body, when viewed ten thousand times ten
 thousand,

Microscopically more of nothing than of substance?
No, I cannot think that through, for when I look
At me, there's something of solidity that could
Embarrass when the scales are stood upon.
Could I really be more space when looked upon as solid?

Then maybe what I saw was right, when in my dream
I saw the universe more solid than its space.
If I could go but far enough away, beyond the universe
Itself, I might behold that which seems as solid as I am.
A dream. Do dreams sometimes illumine reality?

28. Babel

The tower was built to reach a God,
Or so they thought, indeed believed.
He had to be above to be a God, so
The only place you could begin was build
And never stop. Go higher and yet higher
Still, until the day of its collapse.

I hear the theologians of the day
Say God expressed His anger that men might
Be so successful as to reach where He was found.
Such arrogance could never be allowed,
For all of them to be like Gods. Decision
Taken, it came crashing down.

In retribution or in spite, in anger
Or in fear, it seemed as though this God
Had other plans to thwart all future means.
Compassion would rain confusion down
All speech henceforth would be confused
Nothing to one or to another would it mean.

Obliterated across earth's globe,
Communication with his fellows lost.
That is until a latter day, as now,
New understandings brought relief,
As what one said was written down by both,
To say the same in different ways.

The Rosetta Stone and Treaty of Kadesh,
With Linear B and more, I guess, unlocked

The secrets of the dead, kept them alive today.
What provoked this line of thought in me
A holiday enjoyed? Sitting on the bar-stool still,
I could not understand one word another said.

29. Joy

What fun the great creator must have had
When he was making us as one.
For all our bits have function common,
Yet, in looks, have no comparison.

Have you ever seen the one advancing
Look anything like another approaching?
Or, as Ogden Nash has pointed out
For that matter, in the process of departing?

30. Conundrums of the Future

Population was her speciality.
Projection thereof, to be precise.
With boldness she foretold the days
Decline would set in, but we would
Have to wait until the year 2050.

So standing at 2000 and looking back
From there the merest fifty years,
Changes wrought in such a time
In nature were not inconsiderable.
For us, man yet upon the moon had not stood.

True, the abacus had given way
To more sophistication. Counting
Gained in accuracy but no
Calculators or computers
Yet confused the scholar's mind.

If advance is exponential, what
'Undreamt of' lies ahead? For
Today we see the minuscule and
Count how many universes can be seen,
Guessing how many more beyond there are.

New technology commands
Degrees of attention unheard
Of in my youth. Whilst the Hadron
Collider crashes particles no eye, unaided, sees.
The undiscovered comes to light.

Genes, once supposed and now
Believed, tell stories from the past,
As mitochondrial DNA in ancients'
Teeth is expressed, exposed,
And of years past tells, in thousands.

But going backwards takes us forward,
As body-parts are grown. Will years
Ahead allow our life forever to be lived?
And who may, in such a day, afford
To foot the bill in yet more billions?

Man, the master of it all, will
Other explorations have to take
To learn about himself; to live and let
His neighbour live as well. If after
2050 population predictions count for ought.

31. Precious

People are so precious,
Even those you do not know.
At just what point you realise,
Depends on circumstance.

Learn this lesson early.
Even then, it will not save the pain.
But counting others well before yourself,
Creates a lifestyle of worth and gain.

32. A Darker Trilogy

A. Descent

I heard a story once. It was about my ancestors.
It said they lived in trees until, one day, they decided
To descend and walk the plain upright. For food

They favoured vegetation: flowers and fruit in season.
There was a word about the cradle of creation.
Or was it civilisation? Distinction and difference

Might get me into trouble. The 'where' intrigued me too?
Thousands of years span intervening time.
Still 'descent' carries application for humanity.

A handy stone, a fallen branch, would weaponry become
In the hands of early man. Evolution played its part.
Pre and post-atomic weaponry now grant to some their

Will. Few plains are left where roaming can delight.
Jungles of steel and concrete replace the forest home.
Behaviours too could be said to bear the hallmarks

Of descent. Depravity discernibly a growing phenomenon
As population fast outstrips resources' distribution.
The haunting question with which I continually contend

Is the seeming inevitability of descent. Must it forever
Mar the beauty of the forests and the plains, whilst those
Descendants of the first descent continue to descend?

B. A Certain Equilibrium

How old might this, our universe, be?
How old might our planet, Earth, be?
And what Big Bang created both,
Along with many more celestial hosts,
With a vast variety of names and numbers?

She drew a clock-face on the board
Inviting us to tell the time with chalk,
Marked hands that quickly were erased.
Pausing again, leaving blank the face,
A question was put to our supposed

Inquiring minds, as the early days
Of our grammar education had begun.
'How long has man existed upon the surface
Of this earth, do you suppose?
Tell me where to draw the minute-hand?'

'Then, think again and tell what time
First life began, before the first of men?'
A new and wondrous science, unfolding
Before our eyes, exposed us to new thinking.
Our council school was left behind.

As ink in blotting paper absorbed,
So all this new data saturated
My mind and I began to wonder, asking
The questions being formed in head,
As well as trying to obey the teacher.

The suggestion came of five-to-noon for man
And some time earlier for life, say
A quarter-to-the-hour, if that made sense.
The teacher was not thrown and, in the main,
Agreed, smiling at her new protégés.

But now the question, of sixty-four thousand
Dollar dimension, began to rear its head.
For how many, many and many again,
Millennia, might the human being survive
Until, like all companions, its demise?

Imagination on the clock began to work.
The hands upon the face began their
Circumnavigation, at a speed the eye
Barely could conceive. Arrival at the school
Next day, still continuous circulation in imagination.

For all the incomprehensible time that
He and she had gone forth, multiplied,
Subdued, had they accomplished ought?
Maybe the greatest skill that, combined
They managed to conceive, was self-destruction.

Wherein was love, compassion, mercy,
Tenderness and that self-sacrifice which
Said, 'there is no choice, no question
To be faced, for I will die instead of you.'
Who found that truth? Who lived that life?

Then all was over, oh so soon, yet an eternity.
Did man find how it began? Did he find

His 'standard model particle physics' that
Could be extended to all matter in the universe,
Holding it in understandability, giving sense to all?

C. Ascent

Not given to 'prediction' prevented no
Contemplation of the future. What might be tens
Of millions of light-years from now, as planetary
Circumnavigation of a lifeless sun has seen
The bright earth in dullness dressed and, in
Decay, cease to be a cradle of created life
In a distraught universe devoid of ought: once thought
To abound but now known to have been 'exception' to the
    rule.

Was it a day? It could have been a night.
For there was no natural light remaining in the
Planetary orbiting now, in the prophesied decay that
Haunted generations. The last spaceship to leave
The dead atmosphere of earth, ascending
On its journey to the distant galaxy, where mere
Mortals now colonised the heavens in cocoons of
Life, needing no propagation as all forever live.

No ark of 'two by two' to proliferate and multiply
The causeway of the stars, where Milky Way
Became only another place to leave odysseys
Of space and time. No Babel tower to reach beyond.
For they were there and no God had yet been found.
Did the command remain the same? 'Go forth and multiply.'
'Subdue,' but not the blue planet sometime called Earth,

Nor near neighbours of Moon and hostile planets.

No one was left to witness this departure.
Death and decay had done their work, deprived
Of light and heat and life itself. When ageing, now
For all time subdued, had seen the 'one-son,
One-daughter' legislated policy' give way to none.
As all disease and sickness long since banished,
Remaining were the ageless ones who could not pass
Away, condemned to an eternal destiny of dead life.

Did they carry, in their capsule, concepts?
Compassion, pity, kindness, selflessness and love.
Alas, they had no remembrance of these as
Collective consciousness had, millennia ago, left these
Behind, along with emotions that once had all the
Motivational power to win the futile war; where few
Contrived to control the many in servitude, as
Sages said it had always been but none remembered.
They had a clock of such complexity it cannot be
Described, for its ability was to see before, behind and
Sideways too, as it explored the other seven dimensions.
But the forbidden thought, that triggered contemplation
Of the chronometer, can only be conceived in looking
    forward.
Did one stand on that last day and do that which was
Unheard? Remembering a distant saying about turning back
The clock? Was there a longing born to do just that?

There was a day when the last disease was dead; when ageing
Was no more; when fighting stopped forever and when
The last child was born. Need, the mother of invention,

Provided every answer. Nutritional needs had passed to
Pills and no one wanted money, as all provision was to hand.
You could not claim a birth for perfection formed
A cosy placenta cocoon; and death had long since died.
You were 'you' and would forever be, as chosen by
 termination.

Oh, they had often been and come back, to tell such tales
Of time-travel, where the speed of light no longer
Was the barrier once believed. Dimensions turned
Tomorrow into Today, and Yesterday just never 'was' until
You brought it into being because you 'were'. Years ago
Were yet to be, but no confusion reigned. For here
Familiarity was a given and no new learning had existence,
As all was in its place and knew it, both after and before.

Just as the poet had most assuredly begun and inevitably
Would end, so too his poem posited an initial word and, in
Finality, would find another. Here in future's forwardness,
Existing in the present could be said not to have begun
And therefore could not end. It created a dilemma. It was,
And was not, in one breath; could not be created for
Its existence did not exist. So here's my conundrum: its
End, having not begun, has left no struggle to conclude.

33. Raining Love in Aid

I have climbed into the bomb-bays of the planes
Designed for the deadly destruction of war,
Enabling rain of death and gross disfigurement
To fall, unseen in coming when escape is far too late.

I feel a sickness and despair at my being's core.
Conflict: to count on the fingers of one hand no
Longer has potential, for another hand is needed,
And toes, two feet as well, to count the conflagrations.

Why not a mass modification to those aircraft holds?
To allow humanitarian aid rain down upon the unsuspecting,
In their endless flight to safety: security unfound.
The danger there that hearts and minds might change.

But who would vote for one whose policy proclaimed
A war of peace, for those for whom our tears today are shed?
She, or maybe he, could never stand on such a manifesto.
The only one who did died doing so, birthing resurrection.

34. I Looked Out of My Window

The barren branches bend before the wind.
In synchronised splendour they sway.
Pirouetting in perfection, pausing not.

Their unheard melody delights the sight.
No buds, no leaves, no blooms, bear
Testimony to the trees autumnal attire.

Sap has silently subsided 'til the spring.
Winds winter pruning of dead wood begins.
Snow may those slender branches yet subdue.

Spring's potential of green profusion awaits
The one whose seen it all before as
Seasons come and seasons go their tale to tell.

I'm somehow glad that we were not made that way.
Our spring lasts longer than a season.
Sap subsides but only as the years progress.

The brightness of the bloom in brides
Takes a life time to fade into the autumn glory
Of the beholder's sight as he whispers love.

35. Seeing Leaves in Autumn

Whose hand, the golden weft and warp
Of autumn leaves, patterned perfection
Beneath the beech and sycamore?

Whose eyes discerned that green could
Fade and in its death throes release
A spectrum, rainbow in perfection?

Whose thought, with you and me in mind,
Released white light to be shattered in
The prism from invisibility to what we see?

Gratitude is mine to give as generously
As I received, with sight and sound, and
Touch and smell not excluding taste as well.

36. Barlow, His Name and Bertha Hers

He was blind and he was old,
And had passed his ninetieth. year.
What was missing in his life, though
Not often told, for no particular reason,

Was his love of life to hear the perorations
Preachers proclaimed, sermon upon sermon
Sunday after Sunday both morn and even hour.
I know because I caught her writing earnestly.

That is his daughter, put to the college,
Imperial, that is. Makers of Fine Typewriters
Our computers long replaced, with only
Qwerty carried forward for continuity.

Before her fingers were allowed
To touch the sacred keys, brain and
Hands in harmony, practiced by the hour,
Something by the name of Shorthand.

That skill, now perfected, by years
Of faithful service, each Sunday found
Employment in what the Parson said
As signs and squiggles to paper imprinted.

For entertainment in the week, before
The dreaded telly, she reached the stool.
When all was set, the written word of
Preacher, was brought to life again.

And so this very Sunday. not word for
Word for me. No skill, no longer taught
Employed. Just a thought was captured.
'Destination is God's determination'.

This week, with all its entertainment,
Is going to be interspersed with a
Congenial thought. that if my destination is God's
Determination, then chances are I'm safe

37. After the Floods

Blue the skies, no cloud in sight.
Warmth, lost to summer, early returns
As only a week of March has passed.
We fast approach the Ides. That
Fateful day for Caesar bids 'beware'.

Birds with loud and brazen song
Bid human conversation cease.
This is their day. This is their morn.
We have no right to trespass on their
Pristine pleasure. Still 'beware' the Ides.

'Ne'er cast a clout 'til May be out,'
Was Gran's distillation of dress code.
So school day clothes could weigh
Young lives down when early shone
The sun. So, still, 'beware' the Ides.

38. Morning Movement

Sitting on the bedside, just after eight this morn
I reached down low and grasped my pants,
To begin the dressing process, when disturbed
Was I by a very strange commotion.
The bed began to rock and roll as did, the walls,
The chest of draws, and all else in the room.
Suddenly I realised it was a little tremor, having
Nothing more or less to do with pulling pants up higher!

39. Attainment

Nothing to do with me. All to do with Him.
Ransomed:
That once for all accomplished deed.
Giving me eternal security and destiny.
Healed:
That elusive condition of constant longing.
Giving me eternity's declaration of my status.
Restored:
That fact of my being, no maybes.
Giving truth its place in my predicament.
Forgiven:
Tells me what I am, not what I might be.
In its simplicity Henry Lyte captured all.
Leaving us to encourage the soul in his words,
'To praise the King of Heaven.'

40. It's Long (The Nile That Is)

There is only one for me. Though captivated by the
Amazon in youth, no expectation or opportunity ever
Came my way for exploration. The tribes, the people
There held fascination, yes. But another captured me.
The Nile.

Looking long from Google and measurement approximate,
Some six thousand six hundred and all but fifty
Kilometres the experts say and then for countries
Ten to pass through, something here is quite remarkable.
The Nile.

Once in ages past, other pundits say, it flowed from North
To South. However, came the day in some far off climactic
Calamity that its flow reversed and South to North.
The waters were reversed in flow to create anew.
The Nile.

For banks it boasted a fertility of inundation which then
Draws you into deserts, the domain of Seth, who with
His malevolent wiles, ensnares the unsuspecting.
Or so those far off Pharonic pantheon of Gods decreed.
The Nile.

From whence and when Homo Sapiens, or even their
Precursors, first encountered the beauty and the dangers
Of floods and sands and seasonal changes of former
Savannah greenness, speculation continues to abound.
The Nile.

Pressures for tomorrow's meat and grain set migrations
In motion as Nabta Playa continues to demonstrate.
Maybe from the South some moved North, yet others
From the East or West have been envisaged arriving.
The Nile.

No, this was no mere river flowing North from the rain
Drenched mountains in the deep deep South, confined
To banks that curtailed its course for several thousand
Miles with twists and turns and cataracts combining.
The Nile.

After the mighty thunderstorms chastened early
Man in places far away, a thousand miles downstream
A new dilemma predicated his existence in form of
Rising water, creating flood plains of fertility and fatality.
The Nile.

Where could he live? Where might he die? Deadly
Inundation could wash away a home created like the
Castle of a child upon sand subjected to the tides,
Pulled by gravitational forces yet to be understood.
The Nile.

There only ever was one answer, where to put your home.
It could neither be the desert nor the river bed. When
Ancestral wanderings ceased, as crops were cultivated.
Cattle, corralled, and community birthed, it was the Edge.
The Nile.

Season determined whether desert edge or river edge.
Pharaohs decreed its reliability, measured and raised

Taxes by its rise and fall, whose marks still testify.
And every year all traces of human habitation gone.
The Nile.

So, just beyond the Edge we late comers search, to
Find what stood the test of time and water. Rewards
Are manifold as edifice on edifice concede secrets.
The dead disclosing such knowledge that we have.
The Nile.

One of the greatest civilisations the world has ever
Seen was birthed along its upper banks, whose favoured
Fertilisation resourced in abundance the sustenance
Needed for good and great to rise from deserts sand.
The Nile.

The earliest days, still being uncovered in our day
Disclose the evidential truth through remaining graves
Whose acres more have yet to tell of skills to amaze
Modern technological man who struggles with their tools.
The Nile.

Entrance and egress to the desert the four by fours
Have conquered. And the decadence of cruiser up or
Down the river relaxing in Jacuzzi still has its call
From Dahabeyah days to diesel consuming giants.
The Nile.

But I would bid you venture a little further than the
Current cultivation of the ever expanding banks that
Benefit or otherwise from controlling dams both one
And two, which changed for ever the peasant's life.

The Nile.

Here the rock art, from prehistoric swirls, through
Pharonic hieroglyphs to contemporary spray can art,
The work of desert drivers whose masters marmalise
The very craft for which we look, exploding rocks for roads.
The Nile.

Animals abound. The symbolic of status and power
Are mingled with the every day. Hunting scenes
Crowd rocks with dog and armed men in pursuit of a
Whole range of bovine characters, also gazelle .
The Nile.

Domestication at some date and harnessed to the
Plough, some beasts strain to till the soil. Alongside,
As well as interspersed, are savanna stock of Ostrich,
Hippo, lion, cheetah, giraffe and majestic elephant.
The Nile.

Then come ships of the desert, by that I mean the boats.
Not just one here and there but in great quantity.
Their size and shape and purpose, their patination
Is there for all to see, admire and wonder at.
The Nile.

Thinking why I should be surprised, thoughts
Began to form when suddenly it seemed so natural.
Life on the Edge in boats might well be lived twixt
Red Sea and the fresh blue waters flowing serene.
The Nile.

Yet Battle Ships manned with a mighty crew pulling
Hard the oars, then, with rope attached pulling
Proud ships across the sands. Is invasion here? From
Across the sea a far off continent conveying culture?
The Nile.

Boats allow survival, moving over waters of death,
Where destruction always lurks beneath a tranquil calm.
They provide security during inundation when banks
Of definition have long since disappeared, only to return.
The Nile.

They are necessities invention as well as conquerors craft.
Conveying the living and the dead, even to the great
Plumed God's of stature vast, to strike the fear
In any other's Gods to be encountered in the unknown.
The Nile.

They are still there upon the rocks engraved in stylish
Patination along with all the exquisite desert palette
Contents. An ancient sistine display of greater Angelo's
Dimensions, talented, skilled, to match that of any Master.
The Nile.

What myths and legends there displayed. Do they
Differ from latter day depiction of creations story,
Or conquerors territorial claim, portraying Gods in
Man's disguise, to say its mine, though I came not first?
The Nile.

Maps are there as well as hieroglyph direction to the
Mine. Does Wapwaet still point the way beside the

Bedouin's noose declaring water in a well close by?
Yet rock truth portrayed is found worldwide.
The Nile.

Wadi wandering wonderfully lights the mind,
Sets racing thoughts of furthest past, bringing life
To ancients thoughts conveyed in art both for arts sake
Likewise for the life of commerce and agriculture.
The Nile.

Carefully recording, collating, positioning and photographing,
The Eastern Desert Survey's 'gold' was our reason to be there.
Others will come with disciplines of dating, deciphering, and
Interpretation, should such interest stir their soul to search.
The Nile.

We too leave evidence of our passing but do not want tyre
Tacks alone to speak to those of generations yet to come.
Looking to those whose disciplines are detailed and whose humanity
Displays humility we look to them to take our understanding forward.
The Nile.

We are filled with hope that may be, just maybe, should a
Family dragging boat, proud with their cattle, hands joined in
Dancing, dogs racing, barking, emerge around the next wadi bend,
Each could welcome the other, though long separated, as family.
The Nile.

41. A Requiem for Yesterday

Not a ball was bowled
On the fourth day of play
As the rains came down
And covers came on.

The Oval the venue
New to our friends.
As cloud upon cloud
Amassed all around.

Lunch early was taken
Inspection came next
All but diehards forsaken
Empty Arena, I'm vexed.

They tell me its cricket.
I'm inclined to agree.
Down four out of five
I'm just left to grieve.

42. I Got to Think

We walked with the Bushmen of the Kalahari,
Dreaming dreams of simplicity and peace.
They showed us how to hunt for food:
Where moisture could be found in roots:
How to keep water in an Ostrich egg colder
Than the day of its internment. But fire,
They showed both slow and fast ways to ignite
Dry grass, to twigs, then branches set ablaze:
To decorate our skin and protect our loins,
To rejoice with dancing and take delight.

We walked with the residents of Birmingham.
Dreaming dreams of how we must compete;
To find best bargains in the supermarkets,
And count the sugar in our fizzy drinks.
To shop around to find the cheapest deal,
Using comparison sites to swap yesterday's
Bargain from our utility suppliers and invade
The bank with questions that might satisfy
Our greed. Then came the dance, fuelled by
Forbidden fruit, observed along Broad Street.

BOOK 3

INTO THE PLAINS

1. Behaviours

On leaving church the other day,
Departure from the usual route
Took me past the superstore.

In hurry to attend to lunch,
The pound was found and trolley freed,
I hurried through the gaping doors
And scurried down the aisles.

The problem was not produce on display,
Nor reductions for the sell-by date.
Alas, it was the people.
Or rather, it was me.

In my hurry, leaving Church
I forgot to leave my Church behaviours there.
So, for a while, though not for long,
Both staff and fellow shoppers took on congregation mantle.

Yes, you guessed - embrace and hugs and holy familiarity
Go well with strangers in the sanctuary.
But try it in the Superstore
And that's another story.

2. Winter Must Give Way

To coin a phrase, or paraphrase a poet,
I'm going to the garden.
I shall not be very long.
Will you come too?

The weeds are there for pulling
As new growth is pushing through.
I shall not be gone that long.
Will you come too?

And so it proved I was not long gone,
For still the wind had power to bite.
Just time to fill one plastic sack
And leave the rest for later on.

Be careful where you put your feet.
The primrose blooms; the crocus flowers;
Daffodils show yellow; tulips seem too tall.
To tread could be to crush the life you came to save.

(With apologies to Robert Frost)

3. Look Before You Lean

What was it that disturbed me as,
With a quick brush of the hand, I
Almost hit myself? There it was again.
My leaning post was smothered.

Uncertain as to provenance of name,
'Pretentious' seemed my first reaction.
As I checked out ants, rechecked to make sure,
Lo and behold, it was true: a Cocktail Ant.

But why? My imagination stuttered,
Slowed; then stopped. For what could possibly
Be held in common between a tiny insect
And an alcoholic beverage?

So tiny, you do not notice them.
Yet, when closely observed, both black and red
Rear abdomen held high, they gain the name
For trying to make even men afraid.

Connections for this arboreal ant
Tell a different story. Upon acacia it can be
Welcomed, and a symbiotic stance
Taken, even warding off large herbivores.

Not so, when sucking life juices from
The host's vascular systems, milking them for
'Honeydew', a secreted sweet fluid
That is life for the tree, or death in this case.

This minuscule invader, far mightier
Than a man with felling axe, can bring down
Branches. Yet, not satisfied with that, can subdue
The largest of its hosts to knees and ground.

Not one, of course, neither a hundred,
Or even a hundred hundred. Multitudes are required,
In unison, to do what is impossible. Somewhere the
Good Book says, 'Go to the ant, you sluggard; consider its
ways and be wise!'

4. More Than an Echo

He, or maybe it's a she, seems to suffer
An addiction that all peers despise.
As autumn gives way to winter and darkness
Embraces the day, he alone can be heard.

All others cease their melodious tones.
Silence descends near the streams in the Wolds.
Uplands are quiet and woods cease to echo
To songs of birds, save for his solo effort.

Long since his companions of lost summers days
Have migrated to climes both warmer and drier,
Questions concerning who gets to go and who gets to stay,
Unanswered remain. Sustaining his song is his only way.

Today, by whose choice, I cannot surmise
He was joined in the tree by an extra voice.
Sign of the season it surely must be, when the
Robin and blackbird in duet agree.

Not yet arrived but well on its way,
Spring will soon harvest a chorus at dawn.
From that solitary song to cacophony loud,
Neither robin nor blackbird need hang around.

5. Conversation Observed

Have you ever noticed the new phenomenon,
Walking around town with so much going on?
Everyone wants to talk to you,
Be it hidden, hushed tone, or out LOUD.

'Hello, it's lovely to talk to you.'
'What time did you say we would meet?'
'I'm sorry. I'm in such a hurry.'
'You can't possibly be thinking of sweet?'

'I think you're stuck up and conceited
And I'm tempted to say more than that.'
'If 'twere not that so many might hear us,
You'd feel the lash of my tongue.'

'Was it morning or afternoon meeting?'
'It's safe in my Palm, but not here.'
'Your mother said she was coming.'
'Are you there? Can you still hear?'

'I'm not going to pay that sort of money
And anyway, I don't have the cash.'
'Yes, it will depend on your behaviour.
Don't expect the kindness to last!'

'You don't deserve to be treated like that.'
'Just wait till I get there, don't run.'
All snippets and snatches of talking;
O2 or 3G, or maybe Go-as-you-Pay.

Often, I'll make some responses.
As for looks, they might often kill.
But the colour and contortions of faces.
'I'm sorry, I thought you meant me!'

6. Feelings

To what do we hold our feelings accountable? When
Over and over, we were told, 'Your feelings are in control,
If you so much as let them.' They wield the power
When you think it's you. Truly, they were born to lie.

So convincing is their lie, it stands for truth.
Supreme, that none suspects the hiddenness
Of all deceit, their conviction overrules. There is but one way out,
Alas, the only one. Never, no, never give your feelings a vote!

At the very first, they will their ace begin to play.
Not only trounce but also trump anything the deal has dealt.
Meekly, but with passion, deep you will reply,
'I just don't feel like it.' Never, no, never give your feelings a vote!

With passion paralysed, what you thought you'd begin
Now unaccomplished, left to rest, ambition lies deployed
On a sea of helplessness; no movement to disguise the once
Impassioned vow. Never, no, never give your feelings a vote!

Letting uncertainty caress the mind, busy brain cells congregate.
You come up with the classic doubt, 'I'm not sure it is right.'
It's now that the feelings coalesce in formidable array.
Time again to say, 'Never, no, never give your feelings a vote!'

Opinions always seem to gather when not even sought.

Displaying muscularity even bodybuilders might begrudge.
Excuses, then multiplied, simmer to the surface. The classic,
'Other people do it.' Never, no, never give your feelings a vote!

Then she could not hold back the tears, for all to see.
What rationale could be assembled that might strengthen her case?
'But, you do not realise, how could you?
It has been done to me!' Never, no never, give your feelings a vote!

'It's easy, and it always has been, for you, but it is not so for me.'
Maybe you were taught it, so now it's embedded in your soul.
A response, now quick to surface and be displayed for all.
'I shall never be able to forgive them.' Never, no, never give your feelings a vote!

Seventy times seven, was the marker set down.
It stood test of time and translation to suggest 'ad infinitum.'
Challenged on a daily basis, or even greater frequency, my response
Must always be 'This one is just too many'. Never, no, never, give your feelings a vote!

When contemplation of an Honours List excites some varied minds,
Both life's latest, and it's farthest, comes under microscopic gaze.
Turn to flipside quickly and scornfully declare, 'deserving, yes, and even more,

Of everything they get.' Never, no, never give your feelings a vote!

Alas, I think the time has come for my white flag to be unfurled.
There is no further I can go and retain what of sanity is left.
My feelings now shouting with increasing decibels, I told you, before,
'There is nothing I can do about it.' Never, no, never give your feelings a vote!

With feelings transformed into will, actions ensue,
How I 'feel' manipulates what I 'do'. Yet when there are two sets of will,
His and mine, there is no choice. 'Never, no, never give your feelings a voice,'
Discloses power at its source, 'Yet not my will be done, just let it be yours.'

(With apologies to Joyce Myers)

7. Choose Me

Mid-March, they said, no better time. So,
Being taken at their word, I dampened down
The soft warm compost to caress the seed.
The plastic pockets soon were filled and
Levelled off to leave a surface smooth
Upon to gently rest the delicate containers of the life
Which one day, as hope is stirred, will bring
Abundance of fruit and flower, far surpassing
The shrivelled fibrous shell of its appearance.

Tipping the seed upon the table top,
I carefully take the pencil and, with moistened tip,
Select the seed to be the first. Gently,
I rest it on the earth and with a deft twist
Endeavour to leave it in the place I
Have destined to be its home; at least
For its first month of life. Incubator,
High dependence ward, or ITU, its all the
Same to them. And expectation is as great.

When each compartment is complete
With its tiny parcel of delight, once again
The pencil, this time turned upside down,
Is gently used to press the seed below the surface.
Then gather enough, but not too much, soil
To cosset and cover the life-containing capsule.
Completion then, the plastic dome; the story
To be continued. But spare a thought, or shed
A tear, for the seeds not chosen.

8. There is no Sleep in Night

Murmuring, as he arose from the horizontal pose,
Across his mind the morning mist of half-remembered
Dreams in confusion, thoughts and pictures passed.
A sigh was heard, 'There is no sleep in night.'

Who made the night? 'Twas he who made the day.
Could not he have contrived a more convivial plan
For human frailty to be domiciled in light and dark?
A sigh was heard, 'There is no sleep in night.'

Reality is merged and can be judged how real.
Both the waking and the dreaming have a power
That tells that both are true, and equally as real.
A sigh was heard, 'There is no sleep in night.'

Where did I go yesterday? Is it plotted on a map?
The OS of such a scale showed precisely the position.
And where was that? What scale could map confuse?
A sigh was heard, 'There is no sleep in night.'

I like the journey of the day, where sun or rain
Enshroud. But, thrilling far beyond the days, are
The journeys of the night, clothed in a vibrant life.
A sigh was heard, 'There is no sleep in night.'

To vertical, with unsteady step, the tiredness
Of the night outweighed the tiredness of the day,
That brought about recumbent pose as he lay down.
A sigh was heard, 'There is no sleep in night.'

9. A Truth

It just fell out. Before the realisation
Had dawned, she said it, as naturally as
If it had been contemplated, planned,
Prepared, weighed and not found wanting.
'When you step out, then God steps in.'

Hesitation is an enemy of some kind.
Its hallmark is paralysis that first attacks
The brain, before it gets as far as legs and
Leaves the adventurer devoid of will to move.
'When you step out, then God Steps in.'

No intimation to say the time to go had come.
No experiential activity indicated.
'Some of you will go onto the streets, there
To encounter intercession in activity,' he said.
'When you step out, then God steps in.'

Could there be words weighed with greater
Truth? Some might call it 'faith', others 'obedience.'
What about embarrassment; appearing foolish;
Deserted by courage and overwhelmed by fear?
'When you step out, then God steps in.'

Loitering was left behind. First in the queue
She stood. Awaiting instructions, be they from
Man, or God, it mattered not. Just silence
The voice inside that said, 'Now is not the time.'
She stepped out, and God stepped in.

                        (For Ruth Paige)

10. All is Said Through Tears

Years of pain had wracked
His frame. Now in my arms he
Lay. So much to say, no time to
Speak, save 'sorry', through the tears.

He went. He never waited.
There was no word that passed
His lips. Now alone, my words can
Only be spoken through the tears.

First a father, then a son.
What turmoil deep inside birthed
Pain. And still it does, through
Months and years, and always tears.

There is a lie out there that
Says 'time will take the pain away
And heal the lifelong hurts.' If that
Is true, then why, still, through tears?

If this were pen and paper
Rather than keys and computer,
You would see the smudge and softness
As the ever-present tears still flow.

But his son's son was far away
When his last moments came.
He was no age or great experience.
Young, yes, and how the tears flowed.

Simple, not in suffering, just sleep.
No breath to move his heart to beat
In strength. Just silence and a peace
To raise the tears no one could count.

To lose a father then a son; one in
Such close proximity that arms embraced,
The other far away in sleep enfolded,
Wrapped in tears his wife expressed.

Thankful for both, there has never
Ever been a doubt. But hope itself
Cannot alone hold back the tears.
Maybe, just maybe, one new day...

11. Here for Someone Else

A lifetime hidden, at least from notoriety and fame.
No flashing lights of paparazzi, no public gaze.
Just now and then, the odd review recorded in the
Local press and maybe the accompanying photo.
Television too would have its place, but long before
All was committed to video-tape and DVD. No pause,
No Play-back to remind a later generation
That was the way you passed. But for whom
Was that way taken? Was it destined in the stars,
Played out on some divine device that, for each, predicts
A path from which you cannot deviate? Or was it the
Sheer foolishness of obedience to a call heard
In the earliest days of youth, when meaning nothing
At the time, simply became a memory? I think the latter,
As unrest pursued like Thompson's 'Hound of Heaven'.
Yet always for what, for whom? To be employed was to
Be invited and, without an invitation, no ordination; so
The denomination devotees decreed. So all was to be
For someone else. And like those departed hence, always
Appreciated more when dead than when alive and serving.

12. Prayer

From pulpit altitude and contradiction, he declared
His topic would be 'prayer'. The sigh was almost audible.
At least it was visible, as shoulders dropped and heads were bowed.
As architects of preaching know, 'prayer' is a default
For a busy week, along with characters confronted in the Bible.

A worthy topic to detain the mind not at all diminished by a
Thirty minutes homily extended to a series of some length,
Begging fundamental questions as to communication of intrinsic
Truth or exploratory investigation of common Christian practice.
The latter being a goal that might lend itself to a more radical appraisal.

I find at this late stage in life, I am still not ready to embark
On a journey of exploration into territory so well-trod where there is
No path; all around is beaten flat, leaving every direction horizon-less.
In days of youth, a wise man said, 'Sit before the empty chair and
In imagination's eye, see God. Talk to him as one to one.'
The day of books came later. Liturgy began to cast its spell of
Security, stability and safety, with its regimented routine, rostering
The hours of night and day. Giving inward satisfaction of not only

A job well done, but also of a job done rightly; in a cause of great
Significance, perchance impinging on eternity - with any degree of luck!

Yet questions never left the mind that oft seemed bowed and cowed.
Integrity and answers, unfulfilled promises strewn ankle-deep,
Fallen from such ready pious mouthing, 'I will pray for you.'
Am I talking in the dark? Does anyone hear the ramblings of a mind
In search of something to say and too busy saying it?

There seems to be a day of reckoning, held back for reasons never
Grasped, like maturity and thought, with some frustration lingering.
To whom does all this talking taking place? The great
Almighty God no less;
Robbed of his distance through His incarnate Son; who suggested 'Dad' would
Be a better expression of approach, more ready to hear than we to speak.
So a significant discovery was made. First and foremost,
Prayer is 'presence', place of the throne, the dwelling of the
King,
Led by the Spirit through courts of welcoming arches formed of angel wings,
Awaiting the Father's bidding as he registers your heartbeat close to his.
So harmony divine originates. His will flows in instigation, answer or initiation.

'Do not be in a hurry to leave the presence of the King,' is scripture's
Invitation. Lingering there enables change to be birthed, as creature matches
Creator in contemplation, birthing activity impossible to have conceived
Before such meeting. Nothing outside His will has access here and
You are released into His Kingdom's confining parameters of universality.

Much silence abounds. Requests are diminished. Speaking gives way to listening.
There have been times when a faint music might be heard, yet no choir
Practice in these courts, I fear. However, the overwhelming experience
Has to be one of change. For one to have been in such a place, on leaving
Means that things can never be the same.
The urge to regularly arrive still grows.

13. Criticism

Many things come easy and slide right off our tongues.
As in the premier league, that pours forth from the mouth,
Criticism comes most frequently rising from the lungs.

Was he amongst the wisest who once said, quietly to me,
In years too long ago and in these moments to recall,
'Take care, my Son. Be skilled in avoiding criticism.'

As often is the case, grasping wisdom is one thing,
Whilst implementing it another. As for criticism, the
Habit, not uncommon, ensures the biter, bit!

The years rolled on, with criticism unabated. Having once
Been taught never to receive that which had not first been
Critically acclaimed, all had to be exposed, that could be self-inclusive.

There was a rumour, once as I recall, that for a while
Did student rounds, that such a thing as self-criticism could
Enhance the character. But seen in truth, it was found to weaken it.

Coming to the cutting edge in the maturing character
There was, and is, a case to make for 'justified' criticism
From which to learn, and grow, and in that wisdom rest.

No place can, or must, be found for that destructive force
Of 'abusive' criticism that cuts another down, and tramples
On the humanity in form of friend, foe, or another person.

Yet one day, the wisdom of the wise man's whisper came home
To settle in my heart. A sad and tragic disclosure exposed a hidden truth.
It declared that what I criticised most zealously, I was guilty of.

Criticism had become a hiding place: a facade built up of many words
Behind which I could not be seen, and least of all the truth be known.
The wise man listened, absolved, released: setting me on freedom road.

And as I looked and listened, I too saw this truth revealed
In lives of righteousness and truth, of uprightness and zeal.
To heed the wise man's whisper then become a goal of life.

The sad discovery, that what one criticises the most
Is often that of which one is most guilty in this life,
Bids the speaker hold his breath and hear the whispered word.

So, to find another way set me on a quest where wholeness
Has come to many hiding low behind the high wall of criticism.
Not in ways anticipated, but heeding a gently whispered word.

14. A Wedding Gift for the Bride and Groom

What can I say today
To our son and his beloved?
We nurtured you and let you go,
Hoping that day or night would bring you back.
But not alone.

What can I say today
To our beloved, our daughter new?
A choice, that if we chose, we would have made.
You who delight and brighten
Our each new day.

I will say this today
To each of you, that journeying together
Through life's delights, and some obnoxious
Or outrageous days,
Has dealt hard blows.

Be free. Be not constrained
By formality, conformity, or just to please.
Be free to be each other, and to find each in the other.
Be free to reach the distances
No other has yet reached.

Be free. Be not constrained
By failings seen in others, nor their success,
Endurance, false hopes or pride.
Be free to carve and to create that which
Is yours, and yours alone.
And, as for us who gather here,

Watching, celebrating, sharing joy,
We will be those who encourage and uphold,
In silent prayer, the dreams we have for you
That, one day, we see in this today.

(16/06/2012. Our Son's Wedding)

15. Which Direction I Should Take?

My hope is not to return to ought.
My hope is to move towards.
My hope is to see His face.
But will that be now, or then?

To kneel at the foot of the cross
Is to see the soles of his feet.
To follow Him, invitation echoing,
Is to gaze on his beaten back.

Looking up from where I knelt,
I brush something damp from my brow.
A glance at the back of my hand,
The redness of blood that just fell.

And what of his back, to my attention
Locked, unable to glance right or left?
Here, blood is clotted and dried
In deep cuts only lashes can leave.

He said that is all I need do.
Follow Him. His invitation, not mine.
What I have seen, I have seen.
And why am I hooked, who can tell?

Feet will be weathered and worn,
Back will be bowed, bent, and bruised.
Would I change, having come thus far?
His face, now or then, will be all.

16. Inexperience

There was a day I knew it all.
Least that was my supposed truth.
A truth I regularly told myself, for reasons personal. For pride?
Others knew it, or came to know it,
For I was wont to give impression.

So it may have long remained, had circumstance and situation
Not invaded the reality I claimed my own.
Her funeral oration was almost begun when the distraction came.
At first, it was a motion, an aside. Then a note was passed.
'Please tell the congregation her nephew has just died.'

She at seventy-three, and he at thirty-five.
Same congregation, same sanctuary, same cemetery,
Would detain us all in two weeks' time.
They did not know what now I knew
And he who knew it all, alas, was quite undone.

Where were the words of comfort, in this
Needful hour of the pastor's inexperience,
Short out of seminary? Stand tall, be confident,
Speak out, and none will know what lies hidden in the soul
That has just melted, liquefied, and drained away.

But there always is the book. The Book of Offices.
Prepared by wiser and more learned heads, clothed in experience.

Those, who have to print committed conviction you can share,
As no one knows the truth received. But where,
Where to find the words for such an hour, and at a moment's notice?

'I don't know what to say,' I said in tremulous tones,
When suddenly it hit me. A wave of sympathy, so strong,
So tangible, so palpable, and overwhelming.
Tears that could not mask my total incompetence
Now began to flow. Yet I was lifted on a tide of solace and support,
Enabling weakness to be strength, ignorance confessed
A virtue. Now I knew I did not know it all.

17. Rainbows

The pot of gold's predicted place at rainbow's end
Has, to my limited knowledge, never been put to test.
Reason's logic answered me with question bold.
'How many multi-coloured ends of that imperious arch
Have you encountered throughout your days?'

Remembering some double ones, and a triple too,
No actual ends were called to mind but place names
Hurried to the fore. Mountains observed in Switzerland,
And once across the Nile, a rare encounter I am told,
For lack of precipitation, I suppose, graced silent landscapes.

Until, that is, one day, being driven home from quiet retreat
In Cambridgeshire, a startled driver looked at me as
If in disbelief that I should shout so loud, 'Stop over there.'
Obedient to so forceful a command, he pulled over into
The convenient lay-by that seemed to have been placed for
    such a day.

The wheat was standing tall, yet having not quite reached
Its zenith for the fruitful ripening process of harvest to begin.
Gold would describe it then but, for now, pale green would
    suffice.
But even that now shattered, reflected in the rainbow's pallet,
Forming a foundation, horizontal for the upright display.

Rising vertically, at least at that segmented circumference,
The bold blocks of colour cast their reflected glow
Towards the lowering clouds, giving the impression of
A contemporary painter's bold attempt to capture

The eyes of all assembled at the exhibition, letting none
    escape.

Through red and orange and on to yellow and green,
Blue, indigo and violet: all were there, resplendent,
Captured by the brightness of the sun, through the tiny
    droplet's
Prismatic properties that unlock the spectrum, otherwise
    invisible.
In awe I stood, trying to comprehend what I had never seen
    before.

A rainbow's end. Its scriptural connotations were not lost.
That divine, enduring promise; a covenant sign set in the
    heavens
For all to see and the creator to be reminded, as if He needed
    it.
Loudly it spoke to me of another promise the faithful one had
    given,
Personal to me and yet for many, 'What I said, that will I do.'

18. September Sky

White storks overhead, disclosed
By their giant V formation, numbering
A mere sixty today, at height of several
Thousand feet. Only from this distance,
A flaccid wing-beat discernible.
Save for these majestic flight machines,
The sky remains devoid of all else, even clouds.
A sight to match such splendour would
Be to see them begin their ascent from
Roost upon the ground. But for that
One has to be in the right place at the right
Time, as I and a few others were
Privileged to be, in Egypt's eastern desert
Adjacent the Red Sea. To feel the down
Draught of the air as they ascended in
Morning's early heat, that helped them
Rise and make their way I know not where.
But they, for all their circling motions,
Knew by instinct 'home', just as sure as you or I.

19. Autumn Watch

The golden leaves begin to drift towards the ground.
Those first to be deprived of sap and lose the green,
Spinning, tumbling, gliding gentle on descent, mingle
With the passing people. Shoppers, students with
Other strollers eagerly capturing the autumn sun.
Faces reflecting feelings, moods and destinations.
Heads bowed, held high or with fixed gaze, they
Go about the business of the day, mindful of the season.

Is there a place where leaves no longer fall?
Where the circulation of the seasons is a
Superfluous adjunct to a life dependent
Not on the planetary system of orbital rotation?
Somewhere I have read of a new earth and
A new heaven, where differences make for
Impossibility of recognition, where time is gone
And business is the driving force no more.

Leaves for healing of the nations never fall.
Night is no more as, with perpetual light, nothing
Is there to distinguish length or number of days.
Sea-sickness sufferers are said to be safe
With the absence of the water, but what of its lovers?
And who reports these things to mortal man?
For some a dream it is and will forever so remain.
Yet for others, it is the promise of the eternal God.

Today the wind blows, not its gentle zephyr, more
Its mighty strength displayed. And leaves?
They rush from there to here, and here to there,

As though some malevolent power is out to
Gather them, in depth, for little children whose
Life before them lies; can scuff and run and
Scatter them only for the wind to reassemble,
Leaving them for those who come behind to play.

Dream, if you must, of a far-distant life,
Though I prefer not to wish my days away.
To watch autumnal leaves their circuitous
Route earth-bound take, is my delight as my
Childhood memory is reborn and once again, as
Long ago, I scuff and kick the leaves in all directions,
Causing them to dance a tune my feet play, rather
Than allow them in peace to lie, all their work done.

20. Please, Don't Step on My Dog

The other day I saw a man who made a dog
Sit down upon the paving stones.
His pedigree was plain, a Labrador.
Eyes so kindly gazed and tail was languid in repose.
All the passers-by paused, to admire his coat of quality.

His arrival had been in a small handcart
As though, in some way he had a disability
That rendered him in some way tardy.
Yet, if you had looked inside the small conveyance,
You would have seen the startling truth.

All the conveyance contained was soft, sifted sand,
A brush, spray containing water, and what
Looked like wooden spatula. Then emptied
In a heap upon the smooth footway, as though
The work would be to re-lay the stones.

It did not take long for the Labrador,
Whom already I had nicknamed Roger,
To emerge, as deftly his creator and 'master', I suppose,
Moulded the sand, dampened it with the water
And brought the dog to 'life'.

21. Surprised by Stealth

The feeding flock, though small,
Flew high from street to sky
Weaving their patterns against the blue.
Down they dipped and, standing still,
I was immersed in syncretic display.

A sudden thud against the large glass window.
Looking down, my expectation was to see a
Pigeon lying dead from broken neck
Having seen his friends and family fly by,
Reflected in the shining glass.

Nothing there. I scanned the pavement
Till a doorway came to view.
There, staring up at me, a strong, plump Sparrow Hawk
Proudly perched upon a pigeon's breast
With talons deeply dug. Eye to eye, we met.

Time was standing still and as he stood,
Hands to my pocket gently moved to find the
i-Touch and splendid picture take. Carefully, I looked.
Yet, before the button pressed, up and away he flew without
His prey, which fast followed him another way.

22. A Dream?

Head still, pillow caressed from the night's rest,
In dreams still lost, the ivy seemed
Intent upon entangling me.

Its variegated form held fascination.
For a moment, I was lost in dream's puzzlement.
Its growth seemed to outstrip its source.

My eyes now sought another truth for me to tell.
Dream seemed to have given way to sight,
Leaving me to gaze alone up at the ceiling.

To that corner of the room where
Outside air-brick led to inner vent, ivy had for real
Invaded the morning brightness of the room.

23. The Demise of the Chapel

Chapels: as cold as the grave.
As uninviting as the undertaker's parlour.
As inhospitable as a restaurant when closed.
And only open on a Sunday, when all are in bed.

Chapels: training ground of many a musician.
Launch pad of many a vocal talent.
Home base for the public speaker.
And only open on a Sunday, when some are in bed.

Chapels: hidden from sight in city alleyways.
Standing on lucrative city centre sites.
Found likewise in village and in town.
And only open on Sunday, when a few are in bed.

Chapels: generating much hot air.
The only residence of the seldom heard Hoel.
The place of peroration and hyperbole.
And only open on a Sunday, when there are those in bed.

Chapels: where overcoats can be the order of the day.
Where collars and ties are compulsory.
Where, in the heat, only beads are removed.
And only open on a Sunday, if at all today.

24. Wind

No limpness in the flags, full horizontal flying.
Tall pampas grass bowed down as tamarisks, too, obeyed.
The white-capped waves of the running sea tell the
Same story, as those who looked to sails
Were thrown along, at speeds defining locomotion.
Today the blazing sun was muted in its power.

Invisible, we were taught, it moved from pressure high to low,
Having prevailing direction, discernible to those who know.
How much of this can be transposed to that invisible
Of all might and Spirit's power, seen, in its apogee,
Exerted in Christ's resurrection from the dead?
Gentle but powerful, mighty but meek; all bending before.

So music is made by moving chimes: such
Soothing sounds that bring no irritation to the ear
Of volume or discord. Constant, dependable sounds
Make contrast with the songs the rolling of the seas make,
As they caresses the shore sand in their irregular motion,
Fold on fold, gently cascading against themselves upon the
    slope.

What music made within my soul as the Holy Spirit moves?
Of God my maker, He discloses life.
Of God my saviour, He declares destiny.
Of God my 'everything', it is my eternal sanctuary and
    security.
Come Holy Spirit; invade the deadness of this impoverished
    life.
Make the music heard, when You participated in Creation's

call.

25. Should I Compare?

Who is he who measures the universe
As Blake portrayed the hand-span in his etching,
Or as, on Sistine Chapel ceiling, Michelangelo
Caught Adam's creation in the touching fingertips?
From generation to generation, man's marvellous
Gift of mind has explored the wondrous mysteries,
Exposing truth invisible to those who went before.
Living in blindness, oft called faith, too early to
Know what we, the latecomers, celebrate.
As of today, are we a wiser race? Does our
Ignorance not exceed that of our precursors?
The minuscule moments of a Hadron Collider and
The vast dimensions of a Hubble Telescope
Create not answers for a following generation,
Rather expose yet more ignorance for those
To come, in the unending succession of the human race,
To declare a knowledge superior to ours,
As ours might seem, to some, Neanderthal.

26. Christmas

There is something about waiting
I cannot understand.
Knowing what I know, certain of it too,
Why should I be so anxious?
For the day will surely come
As each one follows on.
Yet if that day be death, I'm hoping for delay.
But if it is my bank account,
I hope it is today.
Then the faintest of the faintest whispers
Familiarise my mind. 'Where your
Treasure is.'

27. And When the Time Had Fully Come

Wisdom before, gives satisfaction.
Wisdom after, brings discontent.
Wisdom before and after, brings completion.

In former times,
In later days,
God brought forth His Son.

There was promise.
There was conception.
'Unto us a child is born.'

Filled with the wisdom's Holy Spirit,
Active His wisdom in word and deed,
He did not shrink from completion death.

The manifest wisdom of Father God
Brought forth His likeness in humanity,
To be transformed to immortality.

Somehow, into this divine process
Others are caught up, until Heaven is
Populated and love has won.

If wisdom is a lack in life, there is
A way and place; before and after and between;
That death itself cannot defy.

28. Season Past

The feeling of normality returns,
Followings days of decadence.
Christmas and New Year combine
To steal reality that there is much
Security in the sameness of the passing days.
Though 'Meldrew' is not my real name.

29. Ode to my Bed

Welcome, she says, with warmth and embrace.
Has the day seemed long, the hours slow?
Have you heard my gentle call? Now you have come,
Together we can lay, you and I, in long embrace until the
    morn.

Yes, beloved, I heard your call, my body yearned.
Until this time, I could not come and taste afresh your joy.
Labour of the day detains the lovers of the night.
My love you are so cool tonight, let my body warm you.

30. Falling in Love

What first caught the attention?
Only hearts that secret can reveal.
The eyes seemed to collide, but only for
A fraction, a brief alignment,
Until embarrassment kicked in.
But then it happened, yet again.

Who has named, or ever found, the corridor
That runs from sight to heart,
Short-circuiting the brain?
No words for transportation.
No pulses or proteins to move a message
A little slower than the speed of light.

Clearly, that communication is love.
That has the power to reorder separate
Identities as one, in indestructible unity.
She to her 'he', and he to his 'she'.
Forever. Tears come later,
With more from others, making family.

Just as joy comes later too, flowing
More so from others, in ways the same.
Defining family beyond the bounds of birth.
But what of this love, that words
Cannot capture or contain, define, delineate,
Or decree, as they leave the 'rational' behind?

Each belonging to another now leaves behind
Who bore and birthed them, years ago.

From Poland's plains and forests,
To England's rolling hills of greenest green,
What were the links that meant these
Two were destined to be joined?

Coincidence and consequence?
Happenstance and circumstance?
Deep, deep inside the depths of their
Unexplored emotional terrain,
The answer 'NO' is found; unhidden,
Plain to read and understand.

Their conviction captures 'divine' intervention.
He-to-she, and she-to-he, was
And is, ordained from ages long since gone,
Before even time had its beginning.
This 'Yes' was spoken with divine authority.
They neither heard nor knew of its existence.

Heaven alone was the confine of its sound,
Until that day when heaven touched earth
For them, becoming the moment they were party to God's plan.
And each knew, afraid at first to share,
Yet having confidence naught in creation could allay.
Their secret, however much some longed and prayed.

Today, this 'YES' resounds for all the world
To hear, as each one's 'yes' finds its affirmation
In the other's trembling heart.
Looking from one, then to the other, there are
No qualms that whisper, 'Will it last?' or 'Give it a year or

two.'
Eyes merge and looks combine, as confidence is born.

The moment came. Their fate sealed.
'So glad you asked. I was going to say the very thing.'
Smiles and tears caress the faces,
Melding them as one, in love.
Please allow us, today, to share with
You, what lies within our hearts.

True, today it starts, to the extent
That it has already begun, but in that
Famous phrase, 'The best is yet to be.'
To lie caressed, in love's embrace,
Surpasses all else God has given.
For Eve his Adam and for Adam his Eve,

Before the slithering snake disclosed
To them that they were naked!
We hold no belief that God could
Have improved upon His proposition.
The pinnacle, two lovers, joining to
Celebrate with Him in glorious creation.

Advice today will drip like water from
Spring rain. Dare I say, the 'source' of
Best advice lies shaded from the sunlight, in
The shape of the Son Of Man.
His touch makes three. A strengthened cord,
Withstanding all the tensions of combined stress.

Soft, gentle, consciously caressing;

His words breathe life, heal pain,
Promote forgiveness 'till its need is gone;
Sees not the faults or imperfections,
With eyes wide open, you are embraced,
His plan for marriage yet again perfected.

(For Josh and Natalia on the Occasion of their Wedding Day)

31. Yesterday's Poem

When the white blanket of the Winter's snow
Recedes, in its myriad crystal droplets,
Each reflecting, for a moment, what its curves
Could capture before disappearing into soil,

Beside the veins of dust and dirt, captured by
The flurry of flakes rushing on their frozen way
Only to be released, come warmth and thaw.
In later days, a new world is exposed.

The snowdrop droops his forlorn petals.
The golden daffodil peeps out of green,
To test the temperature; whilst the palest
Yellow of the primrose joins them, for all to see.

32. Contrasts

At 89 she still remembered with much delight
The career that captured her love for life,
To the exclusion of a husband. It still delighted
Her to tell the stories of the class rooms of the '40s.

Visits, always such fun, reminded me of teachers
I would have liked. So, on this occasion, I asked if
There was just one incident of which she was so proud.
'You'll be the first and you'll be the last to hear it,' she replied.

"The context was the years of war, with bombs
Falling almost every night, and often faces the
Next day were no longer to be seen. But kindness
Always came first in my class, as you will see.

Some days a young girl or boy would bring teacher
A small gift, most carefully wrapped for safety's sake.
This day it was a sandwich: dripping and home-made jam.
Yet, for me, it posed a problem, as vegetarian I am.

What should I do? I looked, and thought and asked myself.
With the boy right there before me, he was my main concern.
Then it came, in a flash. I stood before him. Ate it all.
Excused myself, ran out to the loo and brought it back.

He was still standing there when I returned.
'John, when you get home, will you please tell your Mum,
Thank you for your kindness and sacrifice, but next
Time, think of all the other mouths to feed, rather than of
    me.'"

The next I asked was 87, with quite a different storyline.
But then again, the question was not quite the same.
For all her working life, she had been confined to office.
There, with friend or foe, 'getting-on' was all.

The question then had more to do with what was missed
Than what might have been accomplished, as day followed on each day.
"With all your years behind you now, is there something
You regret you did not get the chance to do?

Be it in the early years, or in later life, a dream that,
Somehow, always stayed a dream that never found its life."
"Ah, yes," she said. "But only you shall know. Treat it like
Confession and take it to your grave. It's for your ears alone.
You know my love of countryside, the rolling hills,
The gentle dales, the sunlit spring meadows.
You were brought up in the Cotswold Hills,
So I am sure you'll understand what I'm about to say.

From seventeen I'd say, then on to later twenties,
This longing and desire grew, but never becoming
Passion or obsession. No, that would never do. I wanted
To clear the five-bar gate and trespass in the meadow.

Then begin, as through the morn's damp grass I cavorted,
To divest myself of all my clothes, till naked standing
There I could begin to dance my delight before my King
Who made me in his likeness. That, I never got to do."

33. Snowflake

Reluctantly, with delicate circular motion,
He first moved lower, then higher,
But always lower in the end,
As though he wanted to view all he could
Before his final descent, joining his fellow fallers,
All subject to minuscule amounts of gravity,
Down, to rise no more.

Children's hands would gather multitudes
To form a ball to throw in fun.
Others would roll a ball 'till it became
A man of stature, with contorted face.
Whilst elderly, with fearful eyes, looked
At what the collected years despised.
Down, to rise no more.

Warmth would bring about the change.
Alas for moulded man, he would slowly
Shrivel in his melting process,
Until a little pile of dust and dirt
Marked the spot where once proudly he stood,
Bedecked with scarf, stones and carrot.
Down, to rise no more.

The siren sounded. Music to the ears
Of him who laid prone in the winters
Coldness, nursing pain, whose origin
Held an uncertainty, until the paramedics bid
Him move his 'this' and 'that', if it remained
A possibility. 'Don't worry. We'll soon have you up.'

Down, to rise no more.

So delicate through microscopic magnitude,
Each, we are shown, total in their uniqueness;
Beautiful in their similitude; Multiplied in
Their mountainous millions, giving shape
To geographic continents that defy fragile man
A place for permanent abode. Yet, to a child, a ball.
Down, to rise no more.

34. Friday Sunshine

Friday sunshine.
Seems like Spring.
I'm sure I've visited before.
Friday sunshine.

Just which day it was,
My memory can't recall.
Is there a place where all
Days go, never to be found?

Those days can only
Be recalled in mind's infinity.
Visits, by appointment or
Random, all lack reality.

Friday sunshine, please
Return. Make non-existent
Saturday seem like spring.
Friday sunshine.

35. Roadside Verge in Spring

The pallid nature of its pale shade
Vividly highlighted by the intense brightness,
As celandine, dandelion and cowslip vie for
Attention along the roadside verge.
Whilst celandine questions your penchant for butter,
Dandelion leaves brown stains from broken stems.
The glory of the cowslip is the sweetness of its nectar.
Pluck and suck its yellow flower, to taste
And delight in the roadside verge in spring.

36. Princess

She had the poise of a princess,
With retinue as well.
She rode with charm and elegance,
Was waited on in style.

Her coach, a tailored wheelchair.
For escorts: carers, two.
No 'handicaps' this beauty marred.
Forever princess in our hearts.

37. The Bhatia Baby

The Bhatia baby keeps us all on edge.
Every hour I turn to my FB
To find a name, be it boy or girl.
To you, it might not matter.

Save that it should arrive
With all its 'bits' complete.
That Mickey will have no fears
And Naomi no tears to shed.

Delight above all delights,
The arrival of the firstborn.
Perfection held within the palm
And of God's benediction.

38. January Snowdrops

Through the dank, dark sodden earth,
Between the digitalis' dying leaves,
The slender green and white spears
Thrust their strong, stiff, hooded staffs,
Striving to find the cosseting of snow
Or the early onset of a pale spring sun.

39. Ella's 'A's

With grace and poise and dignity,
She stands upon the threshold
Of a dream that only dedication
Can turn into reality and joy.

40. Negativity Fast

The call went out. It is still out.
A fast of negativity.
Build up and don't pull down.
Be the one returning to say thanks.
Let no praise desert the lips.
Bend low, to pick the fallen up.
Strength for the weak,
Kindness in the face of criticism.
It can be done.
But it needs you to show the way.

41. Blues Triptych

Monday Blues

Blue, the sky no clouds besmirch.
Unhindered rays of cosmic light and heat
Cascade upon the planet brimming with life.
Monday weariness detected in the bustling movements
Of the passersby who, going about their business on salted slabs,
Cannot wait the coming of the dusk and darkness that says again, good night...

Wednesday Blues

Grey, the overarching shade
As, Lowry-like backs bent, the
Matchstick men move from
Place to place, with chins in
Touching distance of the ground.
But, ah, the sun just might, just might, just might...

Friday Blues

They are lost and gone to
The great graveyard of blues.
Today's the day as, lashing down,
The rain displays its wetness yet
Again. No notice is taken, as day gives
Way to a long anticipated, wet, weekend of more of the same...

42. The Art of Asking Impossible Questions

'What if?' she said again. Then another question formed.
Is this the last straw of all the last straws?
'What' has substance and can be described, even
Circumscribed, but 'if'. Now that's another question.
It's amorphous, indefinable and indescribable.
Indeed, 'if' is anything you care to concoct, create,
Or even circumnavigate; for all you do, in circles, is go round.

But are not questions the very bread of life?
A question-less child is like a chicken without
Feathers, a dinosaur that's dead and a conjurer
Without his tricks. Like a sky without its sunshine,
A well without its water and a lamp before electric.
There you have it. A 'let's suppose' and you are back to
Square three as your counting goes awry.

Though it could 'heve bean' your spelling. Imagine
That. No need. It is a given. From days of school,
To nights of love, will nothing ever change? Letters
And numbers, just like notes, have ease of confusion
To the fretful mind occupied by other captivating
Conundrums that somehow encapsulate the mind,
Wrenching it from its appointed task, to sort all out.

Should it be answers you are after? This is not the place.
When all is answered, what's the point of going on?
Alas, yet another question hangs upon the air
Looking for the hook for it to be hung upon. Where
Has it gone? And that's another dilemma that
Often occupies the mind, but never captivates the soul.

Now there's another question. What's the soul?

43. Friday

It's Friday: that must be good.
It's Valentine's day: that must be good.
It's raining: that's not so good.
It's cold: and I don't like it. Not good.
The coffee's gone from hot to cold: not good.
Like the Sabbath, does the weekend begin tonight?
And is that negativity-month over yet?

44. Trying to Understand Today's Prophetic

Following the Creative Voice of God,
Speaking all things into being,
Comes the Redemptive Voice of God
Speaking through the prophet's 'Thus saith the Lord.'

As century followed century,
Underlining Milton's immortal words,
'Of man's first disobedience
And the fruit of that forbidden tree,'
The unheeded prophetic call declared
The need for the activity of God
To be given new expression.
All prophetic voices stilled, save
That of John, whose declaration is of One to come.

Now a Mary, infused by God the Holy Spirit,
Births the living word: God's Son, Jesus the Christ.
Now deed replaces word and is hung
Out to die upon a cross. Word heeded
And obeyed, accomplishing resurrection.
No more a voice, this time a life
Is charged to restore, through death,
The completion of creation in
All its glorious transfiguration.
.
Now apostles, those who are sent,
Bearing the same commission,
Orchestrate the divine plans through
Adam's offspring of the 'you' and 'me',
Whose prophetic anointing brings a

Telling of that which God brings instantaneously
To mind for strengthening, encouraging and comfort.
Now to seek to prophesy, as Paul would like us to,
Demands a weighing and a choice.
Is it of God and shall I run with it?
To whom to turn, is yet another choice
And whose authority's at stake for
'Thus saith the Lord' has long since gone.
Discernment is another gift of complementary

Care to create a community of grace,
Whose talent and abiding strength
Is love, to the loveless and the loved,
In equality unheard and now experienced.

45. Spring Breeze

Today the blossom blew in storm of white like snow.
It filled the gutters, blocked the drains, and did not melt.
The wipers fought the falling petals, pushing them in piles,
Now gone, task is finished, to release a phase of fruit.

Is there ought that I could shed releasing harvest?
After thought some came to mind, deep enough to
Scuff through their collected piles, kicking them aside.
They are the self inflicted 'oughts' and 'shoulds',

That cramp the style, that hurt the friends,
That damage self esteem, and leave the persona
Twisted in a deceitful self, to snap and bite.
A stronger wind of will power could do the deed.

46. Today I Saw My First

International boundaries
Defining migrant or refugee,
With all other status in
Between, over flown
Without the need
For visa, passport or
Letter of recommendation,
In their thousands
They invade these
Shores, being most welcome.

Today I saw one.
He, or maybe she,
Did not look tired,
Though with self
Generated power,
Several thousand
Miles, these wings
Had carried this
Fragile form to
Its summer destination.

Called a Swallow,
Numbers decreasing,
Still they come
Without permission,
Their movement
Called migration.
Passed to people
This definition

Stirs emotion
But they go home.

47. Why Three Days?

A question I keep asking. Why? I do not know.
To make sure He was really dead. To
Dispel all lingering doubts that dead is dead,
As I shall be one day?

I think he knew. He said three days to build
A broken temple. He, too, knew how long a Jonah
Lingered inside a big fish belly. Three days? Dead.
Surely, it was written.

And to the man only a cross away, He had a
Word, giving life into the moment of his death.
'Today, and not tonight, in paradise with me
Your destiny will be.'

Yes, His being dead did touch three days. Though
Not the full four-and-twenty hours of our cycle.
Yet, long enough for death to be defined
By burial in the ground.

And then a stone. Rolled, by men, to close a door
On history. Lifeless body, wrapped in long white
Cloth, laid on a ledge another had prepared for his
Departing day to come.

Whose hand rolled that stone away? Whose hands
Neatly folded the white cloth that left the blood
Stains and the DNA? Who clothed the naked
With garments that shone?

So, 'Why three days?' provokes in me question after
Question. Reflection, too, provoked. Death died in
Those three days. It gave way to life. The divine
Intention at the first.

Morning of the third day came. 'Excuse me, do you
Happen to be the gardener round here?' He knew her
Name and used it with effect. They had been together.
As before, so it is now.

I, too, wait to hear him use my name. He knows it well.
And yes, as before, so it is now, save I'm not dead today.
He called me long ago, and timidly affirmative, I began
Walking with Him.

When that departure day is mine and the word dead
Is used, descriptive of my state, be not fooled in
Thinking and reflecting on what has at last o'retaken me.
It will not be three days.

48. Our Guest

He comes more regular than most
Yet spends far less than all the rest.
When every seat is taken and all the
Space is gone he still has all he needs.

Where only cash will buy your feast
He brushes that aside and with a deftness
All his own soon gathers what he needs
To satisfy the hunger in his breast.

With 'ooh' and 'ah' and 'look who's here'
He presence duly noted. The heads in
Unison are turned as beside a tennis court.
Whilst he, oblivious to most, sits motionless.

Then, quite suddenly, an arm is flung, as
Though to brush aside some intrusion not
Wanted here and, by the way, should he
Not be outside with all the rest this spring.

Winter has given him his bright red breast.
And most, who with him come, a welcome
Have, save when the movement of a child
Surprises him, not us. To the hight he's gone.

Yes, why not leave a crumb, or two, or three.
When spring has sprung, and grass is ris, we
Have no need to wonder, where the birdie is.
He's in The Gardener's Retreat for our delight.

49. The Ephelumps of Wyndley

Wyndley waited, wondering with what their intrepid
Man, one Crosbee, some time explorer of great
Fame, would surprise the world of Garden Centres,
Retuning from a new foray, further than Las Vegas.

There was no disappointment when the crates,
Cartons and corrugated card disgorged, to the
Delight of Sharon, Julie, Chris and Natalie, gazing
Through the leaded lights, two mighty mastodon.

Statuesque and stately, still, they stand with
No need of food or drink. Mighty mother and
Her babe adorning Wyndley's Summer show of
Seats for sitting in the shade and slumbering.

Out of Africa these came. The ears give it away.
And the notice is deceptive 'Scrap' Metal or
Maybe that might read 'Sharp'. The sight is
Not quite what it was. But they don't need to see.

Ephelumps, not elephants. for you can see right
Through the tusks and trunks, tails and torsos too.
For origin try Thailand but China is the closer.
With loving skill assembled, watched with awe.

But it's at night they come into their own.
When critters creep along the ground to chew
The roots and flowers and feed upon the seed,
They stumble on a toe nail as big as any bulb.

Taking flight in rush and tumble, unlikely to return.
Fearful stories then they tell to tiny offspring
Cocooned and cosseted in crevices no eye can
See, not even to the seasoned storekeeper.

These mighty, magical, and magnificent creatures
Quickly catch the eye as the daily shoppers do the
Rounds and pause at Gardeners Retreat for lunch or tea.
Did you expect such marauding mammals would migrate?

50. Natalie

Red, the colour of her hair.
Slender, defines her frame.
Beauty, of the beholders eye,
Reflects demure and gentleness.

Eloquent of word, with that
Delightful sprinkling of wisdom,
Spells early onset of maturity
Casting a spell for the unwary.

Conversation, a delight for
Listening and participation.
Missed, when not to be found,
The welcoming smile disarms.

51. Feeling Sleepy

The drop down menu gives a choice
And frequently I find my finger drawn
Towards its use to send my lap top
Off to never never land of sleep.
And how I wish I too were so
Programmed as to find a menu, click
On it, and dispatch myself to slumber.

52. Face to Facebook

Once I knew you face to face and could converse
At frequency of planned or random meeting.
I saw the smile formed on your face and watched
A lonely tear escape your moistened eye.

Your voice I heard, noting every cadence, often
Straining to catch a fleeting inflection, puzzled
By its meaning. To admire the way your wardrobes
Variety enhanced the slender frame was a delight.

And now your gone. Moved on, we say, to pasture new.
And were it not for that much maligned Social Media
So it would stay and you would survive for me only
In my memory. Now all has changed by Facebook's hand.

53. Inevitability

Speeding down the avenue of time, trees acceleration
Accentuate the passing years we classify as age.
And as for slipping quietly by, the cacophony is
Amplified as, that we thought we would not see,
Confronts us night and day, decisions demanding.

That I was born too soon, only my parents are to blame.
But all they saw was war and rumour of the same.
So why then consummate in conception's labour one
More life to help populate more fodder for those
Malevolent minds bent on the submission of the world?

There is an instinct, driving hard for self preservation.
Procreation, could it be? Yet living through your children
Cannot really suffice when you are not there. Anyway in
Old age the floor just gets further and further away as
The future gets closer and closer until the overtaking day.

What's that? No, I cannot see. Pass me the magnify glass.
What's that? Speak up, I cannot hear if you speak silently.
Your lap tops died, your asking me? Do you think that wise?
Higgs Boson has been found. Did I hear you aright? And
Are there yet more elemental particles still holding out?

Time that once had sixty minutes to the hour now
Alas has only thirty three, but it could well be thirty.
And have you noticed that the elderly are always so
Much older than you are. So now to start again to find
What I put down, knowing neither when, nor where, or what.

Pesky past was present yesterday. Tomorrow's here
And I'm not ready for the day before. Confused?
Well so am I, as I've not lived this long before.
Are you aware it is not given to all to add age to age?
Count it a privilege if you must, but I'm not sure at all.

54. Return

We made the special journey
To watch them being fed.
The wait, with grace and poise;
The swoop, with such precision;
Gone, well placed carrion.

Then on the coach to London
Down through the rolling hills
Of Chiltern fame and culture,
Counting was the occupation,
Noting the growing kettle.

Ahead the road kill rabbits, red.
Above the greying sky, interrupted
By the shape, unmistakable.
Forked tail always did give them away.
Red Kites arrived near to Birmingham.

55. Pausing

After the day of bedside blues
Comes channel hopping time.
Out of the many comes the one.
'Religion' must give way for pause.

There he stands or should that be quivers?
The great T D J, my apogee of preachers.
Then Bill from Redding CA. is a must, with
Such power to move and to persuade.

Now that leaves at least another twenty
To thirty channels, spewing forth such
Nonsense, ah, thats a kindly word, hardly
Fitting in such a battleground for cash.

And then I looked and looked again
At order ascending and descending,
Going up was 'International' and 'Gaming'
Whilst going down was 'Shop' and 'Music'.

Not much there to trouble me. Goodnight.

56. What Might Have Been

Not a thing of frequent conversation.
Details of departure at unknown date.
'Costs need to be curtailed these days'.
They both agreed. 'Any Insurance Dear?'

When came the day memory didn't seem
To match the moment. All she could think
Was that he wanted a different funeral
From those he had frequented in is time.

Somehow she was uncertain of that word
He had used quite frequently in plans.
At last it came, 'A Naturalist Funeral'.
'Humanist, I think,' the undertaker said.

57. English Weather

How come that rain, though water, can be
So variable in its degree of wetness?
Umbrella up, umbrella down, umbrella
Round and round, carried in the hand.
Coat on, coat off, hood up, hood down,
That is only for the first few hundred yards!

58. A Poem for Adam (Bignell, That Is)

His humanity
Expressed in mine.
Likewise mine in His.

His divinity
Expressed in mine
Likewise mine in His.

Celebrating a crescendo of humility.

So there it is, Dad dwells in us,
Reverentially called, Father,
Expressed in Holy Spirit,
Invading all humanity with affirmation.

Celebrating a crescendo of adoration.

59. Time Before

Darkness fell fast overcoming light's remaining rays.
The sound of multitude conversations forbad ability
To hear even the most intimate of conversation.
Around the bar the bustle of the buyers impressed.
Anticipation was the dominant observable emotion.
For what, for whom? Who knew until the show began.

Violet light pierced the darkness creating ghost like
Figures as each sought out a place to sit. Quietness
Slowly began to overtake the restless throng, expecting
Who knew what? But start it would, with no rush to
Begin an evening's entertainment. The start was false
As louder grew the earlier subdued conversations.

Restlessness, uncertainty, silence, but not for the
Sacred half an hour in heaven. A readiness was not
Ready. A beginning could not begin. there is a thing
Called time and for it you must wait, even if you
Have no idea for what it is you have with patience
Sat with all the rest. It must be soon. Unexpected.

60. Expect the Unexpected

Phased but not undaunted praying began.
Yes, thought had been given to topics and time.
'Dear Daddy', or should that be, 'Our Father,'
Starting I stopped. No further could I go.
The pictures crowded in. Family growing up
In later thirties. Mum, Dad, Gran and four kids.
On them and them alone everything depended.

We woke, we dressed, we ate, we walked a mile
To school. Eating at lunch time, walking home:
Some sort of tasty meal and so to play perhaps.
We knelt, we prayed, were put to bed to sleep.
Without Father and the family not a thing.
It dawned on me I knew them well, but in
Comparison with God, my Father and His family?

Now there really is much work to do for why
Should fainter remembering still give me
Greater relationship than that of a Trinity
Of Fatherhood in contemporary companionship
All day and every night included. Much work.
More work to do. My family, I knew so well for
I could second guess them. anticipate and upset.

Father, oh my Father, to relate to you like that
Has now to become my burning passion through
This Holy Week and way beyond. Walking down
To to the Paper Shop I become aware that Father
Wanted to bless each business on the way. And
So I asked for that. Engaging Mr Singh in quiet

Conversation held no fears or difficulties.

BOOK 4

A FEW CRETAN HILLS

1. Crete

Vast blue expanse of azure sea,
Interrupted as clouds gather on
Horizons of the contoured Island:
Stately, the huge cruise liner bids
Farewell to Heraklion, home of
Knossos, Minotaur and Labyrinth:
Dias, clarified in evening sun
Inviting travellers exploration:
Olives, palms and tamarisk gracing
Hills scented with herbs,
Crete's legacy to histories cuisine.

Black darkness of the night says
Sleep to almost all of life, just as dawn
Says wake, but slowly, to the rested.
Fishing boats slip their moorings,
Setting out under leaden sky before
Dawn gives way to light which gifts
Colour to the world of radiance we know.
Where land and sky embrace more
And more is visible as detail is defined.
Nothing stays the same for seconds
As earths rotation never ceases.

Colours invade the darkness of my view,

Black to purple, azure to palest yellow.
When, suddenly a crimson line begins to
Form a semi-circle as earth dips and the
Sun appears to rise. Dominant in brightness
But not yet in heat, it blinds the vision of
All else forcing me to look away, almost hide.
Another day is born for those upon this
Gilded Isle. Sounds begin invading senses,
Voices in distance drift around as breeze.
Life once more is granted as a gift.

Here live the descendants of the brave
As many an island monument testifies.
Those too whose statues adorn the modern
Museum and whose works of art stand
With the best the world can offer.
Minoans in their majesty of grace and style.
Home too of Theodorakis, Kazantzakis,
El Greco, albeit by another name and
Many more. The prominence of Orthodoxy
Gives both splendid sound and colour,
Contrasting the blackness of their gown.
To here come guests from around the globe,
For that is how you are made to feel,
With such amazing hospitality offered freely.
Some, to see the rich heritage archaeology
Has disclosed, whilst others, to allow the
Sun to do its best to beat them brown.
Proud is the word that I would use to
Describe my hosts, but with humility that
Draws you closer to learn more than just
A name and maybe a story. To learn

What has crafted the soul of the Crete.

2. Finding the Right Word

The Inuit are said to have almost thirty words for ice.
Could be for colour, texture, strength, beauty and more.
Greeks manage four or five for love. We have but one.

So fast becoming an adopted Cretan there is much to learn.
Mania leaves uncomfortable feelings that all might be worse.
Eros seeks a bed and excitement stirs dormant emotions.

Philos finds a friend. Loyalty is stirred that strengthens each,
Whilst Storge was in a mother's gift bestowed to give security.
Agape is, oh, so different, in all respects, for it cannot be
    found.

The joy, the beauty, the wonder, the delight, is that Agape
Finds you. Hence those, who, overtaken by the wonder of
    being
Found by a deity of love, had but one word, for all was His.

He is the source, as He the ending is. He woos and draws
Intentionally, captivating that which the wise have called
The soul. In His self sacrifice lies life. All I, or you, can say is,
    yes.

3. What You See is Not Always What is There

I looked and thought I saw the familiar.
A migrating flock of beautiful Black Storks.
With a supreme laziness, they moved their wings.
From west to east, gently they floated on.

Today I sat in the familiar place, equipped
This time with my binoculars, waiting
Movement in the sky to tell of approaching
Flocks moving from the west to warmer climes.

Busy about a duty, looking down, I almost
Missed that for which I looked up so earnestly.
There they were in mathematical formation.
Lifting up the glasses to enhance my sight.

Astonishment greeted me as I began to count.
Not the grace of the Black Storks alas, rather
The common Great Grey Heron, moving on to
Wetlands new to find more frogs on which to feed.

Then other thoughts began to follow on.
Times previous I must, with certainty, have
Argued my identification, maintaining a veracity
Unfounded. A lesson learned for future truth.

4. Early On

Well before the first towel-placers
Approach the loungers, to book the day's
Appointed places, other visitors arrive.
Their little squadrons sweep down low
Across the pool, leaving only ripples
Where their bills break surface
As they slack their morning thirst.
Alpine Swifts look to have had a better year.

5. Above and Below

It's blue and hard as I might try
I can find no white.
The painted palette of the sky
Sustains naught else.

Reflected in the pool is blue but
Now white has been added,
As parasols and plastic chairs
Lend their shades in bright sunlight.

Colours can be confused as light is caught.
Heat intensifies their brightness.
Alas for you, the dullness of the day
In shades of grey, tell another tale.

But then again, is that not what holidays are for?
To see dullness defeated in
The human scheme of things.
Or else, why pay the price and feel the pain?

6. Agapi Beach

It's not the glorious sun's incessant beat.
It's not accumulated stars that hotels claim.
It's not the food resplendent in its presentation,
Nor the bars, that can detain unwary guests.
It is, without a doubt, its unpretentious people.

From the highest in ascending order,
(Though linear would best describe the ranking)
To the lowliest of its servants,
Each has awareness of those who, for provision, pay.
All unidentified by uniform, save animations shirts.

Your every need is their anticipation,
As instinct overtakes them and your clear
Expression in their action finds.
A look, a gesture, smiles, no frowns,
Their countenance a story tells. We care.

(06.09.2013)

7. Pomegranates

Where once the redness of the pomegranate's
Flowers caught the eye, and was digitised
For iPhoto's many albums, now the globes
Of green proclaim the fruitfulness of fertilisation,
Soon to be red themselves, as sweetness is secreted.

Beside the pool, the flesh too takes a reddish hue,
As fusion in the sun fills our solar system with
Its energising power that serves the procreation
Of our life's continuance. Were it not so, we
Would be dead, with no offspring to sweeten ought.

8. Date Palm

Proudly bearing their autumnal treasure
Like golden waterfalls, the dates
Cascading beneath the fronds of
Olive green, standing vertically proud
As they gave obeisance to the wind,
Allowing the sun's rays to do their
Ripening work before harvesting begins.

Almost unique among the arboreal tribe,
Their trunks of multi-branched robustness,
Each bearing the pruner's mark of
Winter trim, stand strong against
The wind, unyielding in their stance.
Strength gained from complete co-operation.
A lesson its human counterparts might learn.

9. Pursuing the Heights

Often we had seen it.
In the distance, towering
Against a purple hazy sky.
Dominating foothills, needing to be
Conquered, before assault upon
Its formidable height began.

Four by Fours enlisted now,
To climb the mountain tracks.
No energy exerted, for
Alas, the years had seen
All that expended, in
Former days of youth.

Through olive groves in plenty,
Not yet bowed low with fruit,
A walnut here, a fig tree there,
Withered vines skulking on the ground,
Sudden colour bursting forth as
A wild flower muddled up its seasons.

Now the taller vegetation passed,
Abundance of sweet-smelling herbs
Assailed the olfactory senses.
A pause, to rub between the palms,
Would have retained the scents.
But our business called us higher.

An assessment of the height was
Registered, as below passed a

Buzzard, normally seen by looking up.
Every path before us taking a
Higher route. Bends that tested
Driver's skills, leaving passengers aghast.

Sight of the summit only fleeting,
As circuitous routes took us first
Far away, then around a bend.
It seemed much nearer, yet illusions
Many tricks could play, as distance
To the highest point was stretched.

What seemed, at first, a short
Journey to be conquered, if a
Vertical path was pursued from well
Beneath, now assumed proportions
Of a journey to be measured
In time, hours, or distance miles.

Here it is. At last, the summit reached.
Along its sides, not up its steeps, we have travelled
Far, to get from there to here. Not unlike
Journeys in our lives that take us
To where we need to be; not straight up,
Rather along, and all around again, to travel up.

10. Family

Suddenly, it struck me.
Unfamiliar faces from so many
Far-flung places. Yet, there was
A warm recognition in almost everyone.

You were there, and you were there.
Even the children's faces reflected you.
We were not in the midst of strangers.
We were at home with family and friends.

Even though two thousand miles from our abode,
I saw you in those faces. Feeling no estrangement,
For each day brought new arrivals and
You were there, and you too.

11. To Choose

Like a dog unable to settle to its basket,
Round and round the umbrella,
To find the right degree of shade,
She circled.

Cushioned sunbed followed, being dragged
In bouncing, noisy motion,
As round and round the umbrella
Its perambulation went.

The purpose of this posturing?
To find a place, beside a pool, in sunshine.
To laze, and not get burnt
But only bronzed.

12. The Beach

Parasols made of straw stand tall.
Rooted in blocks of concrete painted white.
Thus fixed, they cannot always turn sunlight into shade.
So those, the rays seeking to escape, must move around
Just as the planets circumnavigate the sun,
Or burn.

The exodus begins somewhere around five.
Bodies that have been exposed
Are covered now in flimsy, coloured cloth.
Passing the strategically placed shower, feet
Are washed of sand and seek the decking to return,
Sand free.

13. Time Passes, as Does Thyme

Oleander, Tamarisk and green Pomegranate.
Gone the riot of spring colour.
Grass, lying dead in golden straw splendour.
Green olives bend the branches low.
Trees that earlier bore figs among its leaves
Have yielded up their fruit.
Still, the scent of herbs hangs in the air.
Crete passes again from spring to summer, on to autumn.

14. Another Day

Sitting beside the sea I saw the
Earth descending, giving that glorious
Illusion of the sun ascending.
Daylight broke.

I heard the wind wrestle with the palms.
Saw the multi-coloured clouds surrender
To the light. The sleeping sparrows
Flew from roost.

Human voices ushered in the day of work.
It was the gang of cleaners, setting
About their tasks with zeal and energy,
Armed with brooms.

Reflecting on the majesty of creation's
Glory, my mind chased after God.
My spirit bade me look within,
His dwelling place.

A change, more powerful than the dawn,
Broke in upon my thinking. That this great
God of infinite and infinitesimal diversity,
Made me His home.

Could praise, from this weak frame,
Affirm my love for the immensity of grace?
Could worship rise from this impoverished soul,
Embracing sacrifice?

From whence He came, a portion of the trinity,
Father, Son and Holy Spirit, relentless
In their desire to include the you and me
In relational embrace?

Yet come He did, in shape and form
Like me, to walk, to talk, to feed,
To heal, to teach, to demonstrate a Father's
Aching heart.

Responding to such love that ended
In rejection on a cross, that brought
Through lingering death new life for me,
Eternal in dimension,

Now a simpler soul sits beside the sea,
Watching the birth of a new day,
With all its cacophony of joy and love
To enrapture me.

15. Feeling Blue

There is no escaping blue in all its hues.
Blue sea, blue loungers, blue towels,
Blue trunks, blue bikinis, blue sky,
Blue hills, blue clouds, blue flags,
Blue caps, blue shades, blue slacks,
Blue flowers, blue uniforms, blue sandals,
Blue birds, blue notices, blue drinks,
Blue every which way you looked.
Blue even when you looked away.
Even as the sun rays beat upon your back,
The feeling too was blue.

16. Did They Know?

Agape, in Testamental Greek, is Love.
But there that is constrained in meaning
Among the other words expressing relationships.
I chose relationship rather than emotion,
For ebb and flow finds no place in this.

Eros, for its passion roused,
Philos, for its friendship bound,
Whilst Agape reserved for divinity,
Relationship, no bounds nor limits set.
Strange then they called this hotel so.

17. Maitre D'Hotel

Everyday he stands so proud
Conducting his willing Orchestra.
Smart and upright to perfection
In the opulence of his dinning room.

Never one to hurry. He walks at
Measured pace, inspecting all
In passing, its place to be precise.
All acolytes in order and correctly dressed.

His individual greeting is tailored
To your origins. His languages abound.
Quietly to staff, but louder to his guests,
The art of conversation mastered well.

And what he does not know,
He asks. A sign of humility
That raised him from the ranks
Of ordinary, now to this nobility.

18. Seen at the Swimming Pool

Uncertain as to temperature, despite the shinning sun,
She braved a toe and drew it back
More quickly than it went.

There were those heard to say that water
Levels have been known to rise
When full submersion is complete.

What other garments might be made
From that frail silk, though small upon
That fulsomeness, a tent or two for us?

19. Dinner

It was not the distance to be covered,
Having more to do with frequency.
Neither was long preparation needed.
To be present and presentable: sufficient.

No famed Arabian hospitality
In dune surrounded awnings of
Colourful Bedouin tent could match
The laden tables - save for the sheep's eye!

Heated to perfection, or chilled for every taste,
Things seldom seen or even heard,
Set forth in decorative delight,
Weighed down each polished surface.

Waiting the advance, from every angle
They would come. All enlisted, and then some.
None were found to disobey, and none would
Take a chance that others might the honour gain.

Many a battlefield such devastation had not seen.
Repeated daily: week in, week out, and
Sometimes twice or more a day, when the arrival
Of the 'all inclusive' came to join the fray.

20. Out of Place

Alone, I'm sure, upon the beach.
No other I can see. I sit.
Not to contemplate at that.
Looking, yes, you've guessed, at the
Back-lit keyboard of my MacBook Air.

Why, when the sun is beating down,
When both sand and waters warm,
Do I, an alien in such a sensuous place,
Restore a touch of modernity?
That I may be with you, of course.

21. Agapi

Engraved in glass the little birds
In silence bill and coo. Be they doves
Or love birds, species matters not.
Here is symbolism of love and care
Exhibited on every pane, to portray
The essence of the establishment.
Agape, its name, its nature, in the
Genes and DNA, expressing Love.

22. The Best of Bars

It was a simple question. Its answer more
Complicated than thought. How long is the Bar?
Is that to the time it opens or how many
Meters to serve? Here, in the land of legend,
The jewel that is Crete seems freely to float.
Not one but multiple bars, for custom, compete at Agapi.
Here Vasilis, Kostance, Maria, Yiannis, Giorgos,
Clementine, Rena, and the latter-come Dina,
Grace the finest you will find. Serving the Nectar
Of Gods is their greatest joy, and ours the delight
As to merest mortals, their service is divine.

23. Gender Behind the Bar

I asked her what she would like to be called,
As she stood behind the bar.
Mary was the first, for her real name was Maria.

But that was not, quite, what I meant.
Not barman, no, I am a lady. Quickly, I agreed.
Bar-person sounded silly, so she stuck to Mary.

However when pushed to be politically correct,
She chose bar-lady, commenting that
Nomenclature bore no relation to the pay.

24. Holidays

The striving clouds obscure the sun.
But the battle is already lost, for in
Its maelstrom furnace, heat of burning
Power is felt and will, today as on all the
Other days, bring browning to the skin.

25. Stability and Instability

The distant isles more distance gain,
As May moves through each anticipatory day.
Likewise the mountains, losing winter's snow,
Recede in haze of heat and morning mist.

Yet neither has moved a mere millimetre.
All is an 'optical delusion', as children of fun we said.
No fun for those who lived, or rather died,
Through 6.5 or 7.8 and even more in later days.

The sun, the warmth, the shelter and the food
Cocoon my body in its resting, reposing mode.
Should, for a moment, I forget my fellow's
Travesty, humanity would surely be diminished.

I would be the less, and surely you, who
Might happen on these verses in another Spring.
Together we belong, and nought that fact can
Change, unless my pocket has not yet been denuded.

26. Name Day

Bed was calling, alarm was set, sleep anticipated.
It rang at six, twas tablet time , first of the day.
Back to sleep for two more hours. But what was that?
His voice sonorous sounded through the double glaze.
It was only six and bed still called, as did his insistent
Rendering of the Liturgy and the tolling of the bell.

Had time moved on at such a pace that the Name Day
Was here again? Agape, Hotel name and also Love Divine.
A time to celebrate, to decorate the little sanctuary,
That bore the dedication of the same Love, to call both
 Priest and people to be blessed upon this day who under
The beneficent hand of God survived all to be here.

Up and down the Amoudara Straight the word was out.
'Yes, they are going to repeat it all at the Hotel'.
'Remember last year and the great spread laid out for
All who gathered at the Church, at least toward the end'.
Soon all named Pistis, Elpisa, or Agape felt they had been
Invited. Sophia's too, if that was your mothers name.

After Priests and Acolytes, with some Nuns in train,
Had finished the prescribed liturgy, the crowd began to
Grow. Few men and mostly ladies, from the little shrine
Began to spill across the grass out under the great awning.
Here chairs and tables were set out beside the Hotel feast
The kitchen staff had lovingly prepared for such a day.

With a hurrying and a scurrying seldom seen at such an
Age, this large assembled host competed for a seat.

Next the competition moved on to the laden tables
Bearing cakes and pastries, of such diverse design, plenty
To quench the thirst as well. Soon retreating guests began
The task of filling plastic bags, homeward to break the fast.

27. Only in Crete

The sun beat down.
The shade was small.
The ground uneven.
The wheelchair moved.

I must have sighed.
I might have paused.
I made the pushing hard.
I sure was tired.

Her only colour black.
Her presence felt.
Her dark back bent.
Her hands were full.

She offered bread.
She brought from Church.
She parting my palms,
She made me take.

It was compassion .
It was love's expression.
It exposed her heart.
It told of who she was.

Bread for the world in mercy broken.
Bread baked with love.
Bread given in kindness
Bread received. His Body.

28. Sky Watch

Elijah sent his servant, four days plus three,
To Carmel's height. From thence to stand
And gaze across the Med's wide expanse of sea..
Blue above with blue below only could seen.
Save on the last, not know to him, he saw
A cloud, no bigger than a man's palm breadth.
He hurried to his Master to tell of nothing much,
The next instruction startled him. To run and
Tell old Ahab before they both be drowned.

We got to gaze across the Med some millennia
Later, only to experience what had been seen
Before. Nothing but blue in all its beauty,
Light above and dark below, shades seen only
Where the sun unbroken shines, dispersing mist
And haze. Seven days passed as we upon the Isle
Of Crete had come to enjoy a time of rest.
Every day until that seventh, no cloud from dawn
Till dark was seen. Then there it was. And so we wait.

29. Adieu

Animators have a lot to give account.
Five and twenty years ago, she to Agapi came.
And for two seasons entertained the guests.
Cajoling child, compelling adult and cavorting
In adjusted costume, to bring smile or otherwise.

Then passed the years with Belgium far behind.
Life and love, romance and wedlock, intervened.
Agapi had become a memory until the advert called.
Crete could become the dreamed of home. Family
Now of Greek descent adding new dignity, was forged.

So through the next twelve years, the guests of
Agapi, and the love for which it stands, experienced
All, first hand, through the dedication of one, Alexandra.
Between the management and customer, for all that
Is of highest and of best, she has contended well.

Now, what was begun a while ago, comes to an end.
The curtain falls. Staff, guests and friends an
Orderly queue form, to wish her well in her departing.
Missed, is not a word that can be used. Who could
Replace the one, the only, who all our lives enhanced?

(On the departure of Alexandra)

30. Changes Seen

Looking down from hotel height
Upon the pool's surrounds
The lounger's uniform grey
Patterns weave between the shades.

Here and there the grey to blue
Begins to turn. No, not with paint
But hotel towels as guests begin to
Stake out the sunshine slots.

Soon all is uniformly, blue.
Intentionally, the flesh exposed
Is stirred by a desire to see its colour
Changed. However pale the first

Unveiling revealed, the inner longing
Is to see that whiteness, to some
Degree of brown transformed.
Many are the methods used.

No expense seems spared, looking
At the large array of sprays.
The surface of the pool, unmoved by
Breeze, swallows beak or the early

Swimmers plunge, has a perfection
Replicated only by a polished mirror.
But when the ripples overtake the
Stillness, the blue is shattered by

Aquatic antics of the water gym,
All seems destroyed along with tranquility,
As silence with calamitous cacophony.
As darkness, destroyer of all colour.

31. Holiday Not Taken

So we swapped,
Aeroplane for ambulance;
Passenger for patient;
Hotel for hospital;

Coast for corridors;
Beach for bed;
Cup for cannula;
Drinks for drip;

Sunshine for steroids;
View for ventilation;
Minoans for medics,
Sun tops for stethoscope,

And 'all inclusive' stayed the same.
Heraklion for Heartlands.

32. Crete Again

Restless I tossed and turned trying to remember.
Are the passports still in date? Have I packed the
Boarding passes? Will the transport be in time?
In and out of sleep's persistent call things impossible
Take shape. Hope deflated in defeat. Shall we, shan't
We? Then the brave alarm says this is the day.
Before night has time to capture day, we arrive. Agape.

33. New to Agapi

Greeting here, greeting there,
Finding Manos everywhere.
New he came to duty's call
Soon to find acceptance gained.

The revamped restaurant his home
With every aspect under his control.
He stands, though that is in dispute,
For here a skill he never mastered.

Ability to appear simultaneously in
Multiple locations is a must he has
Long since acquired; holding too,
Conversations in different tongues.

What he does not know, the knowing
Is not worth the trouble finding.
But as surely as you are there
A gracious greeting you receive.

His leadership by example set
He runs and cleans and calls
Knowing how to lay the table
Clean it too where marks abound.

Some say he has been seen to fly.
Whilst others, will only to take off
Testify. The jacket may a hiding
Place for wings recumbent folded.

A task accomplished regularly. Each
Meal time graced by his suited stance.
Still, but for a moment, as only Manos
Can. The call of duty came for him.

34. Vivie

A birthday wish
For a beautiful one.
Serene, smiling, shining.
Gentle, gracious.
With softly spoken serenity,
She graces her appointment
To make all feel at home
Here at Agapi, the
Palace of Peace.

35. The Life Guard

It was named the year of the wind
When what all wanted was the rain.
Day after day the flags refused to dance
As horizontally still they stood starched.

Yet when it came it did not rain,
It simply fell as though upturned,
Not through a Rose to give it gentility.
But when did fall continue for an hour?

A sight not seen before escaped.
The life guard left his pool parade.
Not to be seen again when all were wet?
Believe or not he now patrolled the Lounge.

36. To Choose

Privilege gives rise to choice.
Choice then limited to few.
Few can choose a place to live.
Birth the great decision maker.

Before the Gods the people bowed
As Palm and Tamarisk do to wind.
Then stillness that gave way to silence
The populace of Knossos Palaces stood.

Listening in silence as Arthur Evan's
High reconstructed painted edifice
Echoes of Minoan Island domination
Exposed in terraces and cliffs.

Not large, but in magnificence never
To be outdone, Crete called and nation
After nation came in conquering mode
Sequential on histories flowing years.

Proud still its people stand, unbound
Bowing to none, however strong the gale.
Whilst palm and Tamarisk still bend
To breeze and gale alike in force.

Living in choice is for the few.
Who has the joy of total choice?
Where could the better day begin
Than Crete, a privilege for all.

37. In Praise of Crete

Its snow capped mountains stand as testimony
To its commonality with all things created high.

Its beaches formed of golden sand testify to
Commonality with the worlds great sea shores.

The blazing sun and seasonal wind testify to the
Commonality of universes and planetary orbiting.

Museums round the globe laden with Minoan
Artefacts testify to archaeological commonality.

DNA, discoverer of the hidden and forgotten,
Now testifies to that which has no commonality.

Here no counterpart with characteristics of
Of humankind inhabiting the ancient world.

The uniqueness of this Island lies within its
People. Hospitable beyond all races of mankind.

When God created Crete He had in mind that
Which would destroy convention's commonality.

The souls forged in this Island's heart holds
Uniqueness. Meet one and you have not met all.

Touch now the heart of very old or very young
And here the pinnacle of creators art exposed.

Hospitality that says you are welcome and belong
Embraces you not for the moment but forever.

38. Dangers of Decay

The younger generation of those behind the bar
And those, who with endless patience, wait at tables,
Find themselves, often unknowingly, looking in a time
Travel mirror that fast forwards their lives, not ours.

The geriatric generation that wobble, tremble and are
Often prone to fall, receive their undivided attention.
Yet they, not giving it a thought, will in a reducing number
Of years, be served by another generation of nubility.

Fast forward the time frame of those already in decay.
What surprises may await? Have they given thought
To what they might have seen or for that matter been?
Where is that written? In past, present or future?

39. Kreta Cacophony

The ambience of Crete is scent.
The ambience of Amoudara sea.
The ambience of Taverna taste.
The ambience of Agape is love.

What elixir this cocktail contains.
Only God's create such concoctions.
As colour combinations also flow.
The clear, the blue, the white and red.

Light then bathes the landscape
As the Sun enfolds it all in heat.
And evening sees the Barman try
To capture in one glass this Concerto.

40. Times Change

The couple crept away, intent seemed written on their faces.
The poise of passion shone through as hand sought hand.
So soft and gentle was the touch when the final climax came.
He to his and her to hers, the exploration culminated in
The careful extraction of the hidden electronic devices.
Face to face they came, glued separately to glowing screens.

41. Observed

She falleth in,
She falleth out.
The bikini is not big enough
To hold natures intention of delight
To encapsulate what appetite and genes have made.

42. Now Made New

Deep inside the aptly named Hotel Agapi
Lies this palace of delights dedicated to the
Experience of all things to do with Fine Dinning.

Being executed by experts excelling in their
Individual arts. Skills are displayed through the
Whole range from hygiene on to that of management.

Chefs delight to tantalise the palate with creations
Traditional and avant guarde, whilst waiters compliment
These skills with their own range of delightful talents.

Your matchless welcome is second to none this side
Of Heraklion where Minoans fist exploited the
Art of palatial living here recreated just for you.

43. Holidays

The mountains waited,
Caught the cloud,
Calling moisture down.

Obligingly the rain
Dampened all
In its descent.

As 'All Inclusive' looked
For space to mourn
Money well spent.

BOOK 5

HILLS YET TO CLIMB

1. Relaxation

He taught me good.
And soon I learned, from toe to fingertip,
Via all the intervening muscles on the way,
To relax.
Release and, from all tension,
To escape.
But where to practice to get the time from sixty minutes
Down to the proposed sixty seconds?

A challenge formed within my mind.
The next visit would see conclusion of the matter.
Not to the teacher but to the dentist's chair,
There to find the proof of pudding
As, with a screech, the drill engaged.

2. Poor Bird

Four birds must escape the nest and fly,
Or else their destiny is a downward plunge to death,
Pushed by the strongest of the brood and often that of
Parasite,

Cuckoo!

3. How to Live Your Life!

From many countries around the world I have observed
The Bumper Sticker craze.
Conclusion clear makes California its zenith.
Yet hard pushed is it by some emerging nations.

Traffic on Highway One, along with many others,
Moves so slowly twice a day
That reading them presents no problem,
When the light is right and pollution permits perusal.

Jamaica said, 'You toucha my car, I smasha your face.'
Whist Nairobi said, 'Be Blest.'
Siberian Krasnoyarsk's 'Keep our streets clean.'
Compared with Cairo's 'Keep your distance.'

Then some longer versions caught my eye,
None more so than in Malawi's Lilongwe.
'So live your life,' the message read, 'that when you're dead,
The preacher won't have to lie on the occasion of your
    funeral.'

4. Appropriate

They said he did it single handed,
Built his business up from scratch.
Many years with toil and labour,
Using all collected skills.

With knives and cleavers, steels and saws
Quickly he reduced a carcass
To its constituent parts. Whether
Ox or sheep, pig or poultry - all had to succumb.

From grazing fields and farmyard pens,
All were corralled and made an exit
By trailer, truck or on the lorry.
'The destination abattoir,' it's called.

Yet when his time came, it was a different story.
With his wife, he'd planned each detail
Of how his passing would be marked.
Save for the organist, who at his departure played

Johann Sebastian Bach's cantata,
'Sheep may safely graze.'
Not, alas, the full five minutes.
Just enough to ignite the smiles.

5. Noah

A small warm hand wriggled its way
Into mine as I stood sharing in a
Time of prayer. Not my time to pray yet,
So I looked down. 'Good morning, Mr Bill.'

'Mummy,' she whispered. Mum bent low.
'Noah is in church today.' 'I don't think so.'
'Yes, Mummy, he really is.'
'Are you quite sure about that?'

'In that case you had better point him out.'
'Look, he's over there.'
'But I can't see him through the crowd.'
'Standing next to the lady with grey hair.'

Alas, Jemima had blown my cover!
And, maybe her own as well.
Perplexed parents eventually found the clue.
The Bible Story Book. He looked just like Mr Bill.

6. Handling the Cup

Attention-like, his little finger stood,
As round he rolled the remnant in his cup.
From vertical to horizontal the vessel
Now disgorged the last remaining dregs
As, simultaneously, he rose – disturbing his repose.

7. Flying

The seat-belts fastened and the trays stowed,
Doors cross-checked and lockers closed,
The cabin crew heeds the pilot's words
To take their seats and prepare to rise.

The runway left, the clouds passed through,
Climbing, climbing, higher still,
Then sounds the dulcet tones that tell
Now is the time for their practiced drill.

Coats discarded and aprons donned,
The smell of fresh coffee tells of
Cabin-crew tasks for passengers' repast:
Release the belt and lower the tray.

Drinks and refreshment soon on their way
As the slender trolley makes its starts and stops.
For the next forty minutes, a new view is ours…
Up air-crews armpits instead of stars!

8. Right Divine

To whom belongs the 'right' divine?
It has been heard of Kings to hold such truth.
Yet cruel fate stores other fears,
As heads have rolled for far less tears.

Did it have to be that mortal man had
No responsibility or right to
Determine rulership, succession
Or one political persuasion from the next?

Decreed in distant sphere,
Where dwell the great divines
Of ancient times and seasons,
By some mysterious word that all receive?

This is to be obeyed. Forth
Has gone the truth that some
Scheming little upstart, once to
Verify his place, declared himself 'divine'.

Not, alas, from scenes of long ago
Such spurious ideas flowed. For now, a new
Right 'divine' has been declared.
All Private Hire can do just as they please!

9. Passing By

Walking, running, cycling – at least all, rushing.
Drinking, eating, chewing – at least all, breakfasting.
The students hurry by to destination…College.

There is another demanding destination, opposite
In direction now. Still to eat, to drink, to chew.
But this time…Starbucks, Nero and a Costa.

10. Sagging

Sagging is going out of fashion!
So information has reached me.
The quote supported its demise,
Though left me in malaise.

Of Irish by descent,
Some would have us to believe,
Of building-site display, as
Bending caused the revelation.

The modern version, much
More discreet, allows for the
Lowering of the outer, whilst
The inner can be retained discreet.

No bending now involved
And, belt replacing bracers,
Only careful lowering can be
Allowed to display the multi-coloured

Manifestations of the underwear
Modelled on the 'coat of many colours'.
They create a new display in fashion
That can cause the elderly to stumble.

11. M&S

Around the cavernous entrance,
Gathered like vultures seeking food,
Standing and sitting, the male of the species
Await their wives return.

The return of those last seen
Laden down with garments of all shapes and sizes,
Disappearing into corridor and cubicle
Labelled clearly, 'Changing Rooms'

Before departure from the desk,
Some token is exchanged.
'Is that to identify what was taken
Or who took what?' I ask myself.

'I'm sure that more go in than out,'
He said, turning from the sports pages,
Having now to engage pictorially
In a 'paper that was not his choice.

Still they come in. 'Where do they go?'
Was still the question that perplexed
As I joined the waiting host,
Almost afraid to release my wife's left arm.

Yes, it was a long time she was gone.
Some gave up and went away, what outcome
Later to enjoy. But oh, my joy. My wife appeared,
Unburdened now. 'Too long,' was all she had to say.

12. Sunday at Stow

Standing in the pulpit,
High above all contradiction,
I looked down upon the sparseness
Of the congregation.

Preparations well in hand from
Probationary days, the order
Of the happening was thoroughly researched.
Time had now come for deliverance to begin.

To say embarrassment is a
Simultaneous emotion can, at times,
Bear accuracy that defines the moment
And indelibly defines the man.

Such was this opening entitled
'Call to Worship' and all few stood as I began,
Fresh from the Psalmist printed page,
A most majestic 'Spoonerism'.

It echoed round the non-conformist
Square and windowless erection
With its pew-polished pine, barren seats,
'Who is a Gardening Pod like Thee?'

13. The Runaway

Four of us, plus one, the driver,
In the white pick-up truck, were returning
From the day's events in far-flung villages.
Many miles were covered at a steady pace,
Phoning on ahead to put the kettle on.

From North and still going South
The main road, in a fair state of repair,
Was lined with trees still yet standing tall
Because of legislation that decreed roadside trees
Must be left to flourish, and not be used for fuel.

Between the trees, damaged by lost limbs,
Was grass - enough to give a herd some grazing rights.
To almost every tree, at dawn's first light,
Was tied a growing cow who, after weeks of cropping
Short, from this growth would some new weight acquire.

A farmer without field, with but a verge,
Just as my Great Uncle began his milking herd
Long ago in the rolling Cotswold countryside.
But this is far away in Africa. Malawi, to be precise.
The 'Warm Heart of Africa' as it is advertised.

Up ahead the traffic slowed - the reason
Not yet clear. We would find out soon enough,
But not enough to slow the speculation. Yet when
Revealed, it was not the usual breakdown.
Before us, a young black bullock roamed.

Around its neck, a length of sturdy rope was tied
Which, snakelike, slithered twixt the cars as
It ran wild, frightened and frustrated.
Smart thinking on our driver's part avoided not the rope
But aimed our vehicle at its twisting form.

He hit the rope, applied the brakes and
Suddenly we stopped. Alas, we were not the only
Ones to experience that fate. The blundering beast,
As rope ran taut, with crashing sound its head hit road,
Shaving its bottom jaw upon the tarmac, rough.
Exiting the vehicle fast, supposing it to be dead.
We rushed and freed the rope from wheels.
Had we but stopped to think things through,
Our predicament could have changed.
For now, this black power house was pulling us along.

One, two, then three and four, play
'Tug-a-War' between the cars. Some see
Us, and some see him, but none see both at once.
Midst honking horns and ribald shouts, our labour's
Not in vain, as with great skill we haul the hulk aside.

Back on the verge at last we look for trees
To use again as tether posts and let the
Grass once more be grazed, whilst wondering,
With some happy smiles, how the owner of this cow
Will feel when finding it four miles nearer town.

14. Well-Chosen Picnic Site

The air was clear.
The wind was strong.
The view impeccable.
Portland Bill, in finest clothes displayed.

The lee was sought.
The bags unpacked.
The cutlery all sorted.
Portland Bill, in finest clothes displayed.

The plates passed round.
The cheese was shared.
The drinks were poured.
Portland Bill, in finest clothes displayed.

The salad was selected.
The ham fresh sliced.
The condiments came last.
Portland Bill, in finest clothes displayed.

Then round the lee
The strongest wind
Became a violent gale.
Portland Bill, bedecked with lettuce leaves.

Not those for giving up,
A novel plan devised.
Both knife and fork on salad green
Kept Portland Bill in finest clothes displayed.

15. Offers

Offers abound and leap at you
From every place you go, every
Page you turn and every switch you throw.

It is not that I must have these things
Whose use may be but only once.
It is the fact that it might a 'bargain' be.

So, what constitutes a bargain?
First, it must be something you do not need.
Second, it has to have no purpose you perceive.

But third, and most importantly, it has to
Cost something you can ill afford, a price
Set so low, you are prepared to give your cash away.

16. Taking the Tablets

'Tomorrow I will take you on a tour,'
The Housing Director said. 'Of all our
Latest, completed and uncompleted,
Developments. As chairman, you should
Know these things.' With that, I did concur.

Tomorrow came. The tour began and
The trouble I was in, I could not confess.
It was the night and, as my practice was,
Beside me on the bedside shelf the tablets
Were arranged. Two for me and two for her.

No, not my wife, but mother-in-law, for whom I did
The nightly round of, 'Tea and tablets, time for sleep,
Be good tonight, God Bless.' Alas for both, I gave her mine
And her's did take instead. So all next day, through
Half-closed eyes, I looked but did not see.

17. Ten Dollars is Ten Dollars

The offer at the Country Fair captured
Her imagination. A flight for ten dollars.
And she before had never flown. Today?
Reluctant he to spend such hard earned cash
Finally agreed. Up into blue beyond they flew.
But when they looped the loop and she fell
Out. He only said, 'Ten dollars is Ten Dollars'
It seemed so very funny at the time.

As darkness fell and dinner passed
The stories and the jokes began to flow
But not from aggravated alcohol, oh no.
Ten Dollars was the climax and, in the
Context of the company, laughter was not
Restrained. Time was late. Ladies had left.
Retired, for morning chores would come too soon.

You see, we were in Africa and its warm heart
At that. Malawi, so the story goes.
Taking his leave, he slipped away, his wife to
Meet in the adjoining bedroom, whose walls
Were thick enough that we could not enjoy
Their conversation. We, that is the three,
Stayed awake recovering from the day and
Dissecting its events. Suddenly, our subdued

Silence was shattered with a laugh that broke
Through the walls and startled us, causing us
To wonder, in our innocence, what might be going on.
At breakfast, early the next day disclosure

Was requested as to what had caused
Such mirth last night that broke the silence,
Sending the Guinea Fowl off in a cacophony of cries.

It was my wife, his confession told.
When the punch line came, Ten Dollars is Ten Dollars.
She was uncontrollable, quite understandable.

18. Matrimonial Symmetry

They came on Friday to get all
Ready for the Saturday.
Entrance, pew ends and choir rails,
Displayed great flora symmetry.

Come the day, her family arrived,
Sitting on the Bride's side, waiting.
The bride too came, resplendent all in white,
But on looking round saw only empty space.

There was no groom, no groom's
Family. It could not be that
They were late, to a man and to a lady.
So, recrimination soon set in.

Somewhere ears must be burning.
Somewhere curses came to rest.
Somewhere a groom and family,
Had betrayed a bride.

Conversations were the same.
Accusations echoed as if in harmony.
The vitriol poured forth
And ears, like blotting paper, absorbed.

In all, it took about an hour to get both
Parties together in one place. Just
A misunderstanding, each to the other said,
As each to separate chapels had repaired.

About what was thought,
About what was said,
Whilst each separately lingered,
Most assuredly will to grave be carried.

19. A Close Call

The hearse pulled up.
The Crem doors parted.
The coffin, raised by bearers.
The organist filled space with music.
The minister stood in place.

Down the aisle, the procession processed.

Something was needed to complete
The scene. No mourners were apparent.
Time and tide are said to wait for no man.
The same applies to funeral arrangements.

Further down the aisle, the procession processed.

The moment of committal approached.
Still no mourners had arrived.
The minister's finger hovered over the button
That would send the coffin on its way.

When down the aisle, another procession processed.

The doors flung wide and in they rushed,
The mourners from pub. Drinking the deceased's
Health, in explanation they announced, the
Rugby club clock was nowhere to be seen.

Now the procession could process.

Upon the coffin, the wreath was placed.

The journey could begin.
When, to the start, the minister returned,
The organist accompanied him.

The final procession processed, until the curtains closed.

20. Wrong Hole

Through the manicured maze, the undertaker undertook.
Hearse and the following cars, in solemn sequence slowed.
From behind the glazed screen a tapping sound was heard.
Followed by a plaintive cry, 'Why are we stopping here?'

'You see the mound, madam. The hole is out of sight.'
'That's not our Sis,' the customer, who is always right,
Cries out. 'She's over there, beneath that tree. We chose
The spot together.' 'So sorry Mam, we'll be back tomorrow.'

21. Time Was Running Out

Upon the highest spot, the crematoria stood.
Resplendent in its refit, complying EU Law.
The first snow of the season silently caressed
Mass graves, frost now made to sparkle.

Time taken to arrive along the salted roads,
Allowed for. Funerals - fifteen to twenty minutes with
Or without hymns, and no time for an oration.
Stand, sit and say the grace - and they are gone.

Thus anxiety, weighing heavy now, began
To urge a visit to the cold without. Cassock-less
I ventured forth, scanning the whiteness for
A cortège. 'One Hearse and two to follow sir?'

Some movement at the bottom gate, attention
Caught. Yet nothing to disturb the serenity and peace.
But wait a moment. Something seems to stir.
Back to the same spot, attention is again drawn.

And, yes, things had moved on, but not apace.
A hearse had come into view with back wheels
Traction-less, its only forward motion was provided
By the mourners. Two empty, following cars.

Why, on arrival beneath the sheltering awning,
Did they all decide to get back in and then,
With dignity, disgorge from car and firmly grasp
The coffin, not daring to shoulder arms?

22. Blest Rain Upon the Saddest Day

Outside the cemetery chapel, the mourners stood in rain
Awaiting the grand arrival of the deceased to be shouldered in.
Approaching what seemed to be the principal damp mourner,
I suggested all go inside and wait towards the back so,
When the coffin was bourn in, they could follow on, not wetter.

In they went, glad of advice given, unaware of the future event.
Warm now and able to chat, in little groups they gathered whilst
The hearse, arriving on time, slowed a little then stopped content.
The bearers took up their stations aligned at opposite sides.
As the coffin was slid from the front, each grasped the brass handle tight.

It was then unexpected expected and the unbelievable believed.
The bottom of the coffin fell, the deceased descended to the floor!
In a simple act of compassion, the redundant shell was put down,
Restoring decorum and modesty as all was laid out on the ground,
Giving simple dignity to a calamity not seen for many a year.

The tall, black and straight silhouette approached through the rain.

'Would you mind going into the mourners with a message?' he said.
'Be kind enough to tell them that the arrival of the deceased
Will be a little bit delayed, on account of some circumstances
Not foreseen.' Without a moments hesitation, the answer was 'no'.

'You dropped the dead on the driveway. Now, tell it to their faces.
It was I who invited them to shelter. It's your turn to tell the disgrace.'
'Ladies and gentlemen,' the drowned-looking man in top-hat began.
A five minute oration followed, of which any preacher would be proud,
Explaining that, 'no, there was no real problem, Jack would be back.'

23. Camping Catastrophe

Every place was taken, almost before
The notice was pinned in its place.
Term over and the rush to book
The usual camp away into the highlands.

Teenagers, excited, made all their plans,
As did George, much loved teacher in charge,
Who efficiently organised logistics.
Tents, sleeping bags, transport and food.

The site was gently undulating.
Tents, erected quickly, the campers
Headed for the brook, beyond which lay
The railway track with its numerous sidings.

Evening came. The chores were done.
The meal was both cooked and consumed.
To their tents, the tired teenagers repaired.
Two to a tent, it had all been agreed before.

Beside the glowing embers, replete
From welcome food, George looked around.
Each to his tent had gone. But he?
He had forgotten his own needs.

So tent-less, yet ever resourceful,
He found the bridge that crossed the brook,
That accessed the rails and led to sidings
Full of empty wagons all hooked up.

Finding one with door ajar and straw inside,
He snuggled down, settling for the night,
Which, when the morning broke, found him
Many a mile away in glorious Glasgow.

24. Harvest Festival

As from the first, six-thirty was the time.
The Law of Medes and Persians has to stand.
No time change for a nonconformist liturgy.
And Harvest Festival too, will forever be.

In the urban rurality of the inner city
We celebrated the allotment's pride.
Pumpkins, parsnips, plums, pears and apples
Adorned the dissenter's Baptist chapel.

The geographical location brought regular
Surprises, some worse for drink or drugs.
All, too, remember when the 'Chippendales' arrived.
The weeks it took to sort emotions out.

The uninvited wedding guests and
Those who felt communion wine had
Not been exposed to alcohol, so wouldn't
Come again. Just like the sermon tasters.

With her white enamel bucket in one hand,
Bogs of belongings in the other, she climbed
The three steps and made her entrance,
Pausing to admire the display, or so we thought.

Before you could begin to sing a hymn,
She put her bags aside. Without a word of
Please or thank you, proceeded to fill her bucket
Full of fruit from the carefully constructed display.

Carrying it down the aisle, she found a pew.
Guarding the bucket beside her, she began to
Empty her bags, draping her wardrobe
Decoratively along the seats back, almost done.

Or so we thought, as again she delved into a bag.
This time producing a large alarm clock.
Loudly, she wound it up with exaggerated
Motion, then placed it on the pew's shelf before her.

The choir came in and saw the sight.
Climbing the pulpit stairs, I looked down,
Quickly locating the source of the loud ticking
Bouncing its echo round the finest sanctuary.

On the offering plate, she placed a plum
As all eyes where on her now, watching to see
What next surprise she had in store. As
I, for one, held my breath, awaiting the alarm!

25. Waiting for Muriel

Waiting would hardly be the word to use,
If it was meeting you had in mind.
But avoidance, now that would be a different game.

No matter where you were, no matter where you are,
A target you become for conversation. Subjects
You would never choose become exposed.

Sitting at the bus stop, 'I'll come too!' she said.
The bus arrived. I got on and she came too.
The stop I chose to make escape was not disclosed.

Then in Tesco, can you believe? I heard about her past.
Too complex to record and libellous at that.
Had I her husband been, she might be looking still.

The staff had no idea why she came. Perhaps it
Was the warmth, or again, the people paying in or taking out,
To engage in frankest conversation.

From the Bank to Building Society, not even the
Chemist could escape. Customer's chairs
Were a convenient stance to ask the staff to stop.

'How old are you? Where do you live?
Oh, that's a lovely name. I had a cat called that.
Yes, I'll go home for tea, but don't like bed.'

So she haunts the precincts shops, subject of many a smile.
Be careful as you enter, she may be sitting there,

Ready to come close again and chat about her past.

26. Motorway Joy

The fields their autumn mantles donned.
The verges losing green,
Leafless branches aided distant view.
Red rose hips and haws could counted be,
As we sat motionless, or almost, in unmoving lanes
Of motorway mayhem, for four hours and more.
We left at eight, back home at three.
Been nowhere - only seen what speed denied.

27. Outlook

Darkness descends in daylight.
White streaks obscure the view.
Hailstones increase in size.
In warmth, I sit sipping latte.
Will it pass before I leave?

28. Stopped for Speeding

Darkness engulfed the 'forty-five' as rain lashed down.
Headlights, powerless to penetrate the wet reflections
Allowed for utter concentration. So absorbed I saw
Not the blue revolving light. It pulled out, flashing past.
It overtook, slowed and to a standstill came. So did I.

'Do You know what speed you were doing sir?' gently he
    inquired.
'Well no officer,' I honestly replied. 'Over the limit Sir.'
He said, 'I'm afraid it will be a ticket now.' And so he began
To write. Through the open window, he thrust the finished
Work, whilst I was left to contemplate my carelessness.

So close to home, so soon indoors, I had to have a plan.
In the congregation, the young constable looked up.
He, too, now at home, received a call from me.
Explaining all the circumstance, I asked what I should do.
One thing alone he said, 'Write to the Chief Constable.'

Cast all your care on Him and tell the truth. It's all that
You can do.' Then began the task of crafting an epistle
That might capture his attention, stir compassion and
Save me both points and pounds. My mind began the
Journey back to the church car park - where it all began.

Premises now empty, I was last to leave. Through the
Lashing rain, I ran to the car and clambered in. Turning
The key the engine did not let me down but when I switched
The wipers on they failed to move. The dipped lights
Worked but with visibility so restricted I began to ponder.

Fuses…that would be the problem. Accessed inside
Would mean I could keep dry. I found the spares but alas
For me, there was none of power to replace the windscreen
Blades. Looking along the coloured rack, I noticed two the same.
So lights for instruments could do the job, and clear the screen.

Making the switch, I settled in to journey home in darkness.
Little wonder then that, when asked what speed I
Might be doing, I had no idea. Glad that I could see the road
In front of me rather than the dials, I almost made it.
So began the compilation for the chief, telling nothing but the truth.

The letter came after a week or two. 'It's no excuse for speeding
Sir, but I don't think you made the story up. So, on this occasion
I will take no further action - just give you a warning,
Inviting you to take more care and control your speed.'
It paid to tell the truth and save both points and pounds.

29. Pop

Seated one day in the garden
Enjoying our afternoon tea,
Suddenly peace was shattered
What could the explosion be?

Soon to discover, as
High o'er the hedge,
Standing guard in between,
A cork from Champagne

Sailed into our view,
Boldly landing on table
With its cakes, cups and
Spoons all neatly displayed.

Idea, not long in formation, came
A label was quickly applied,
Then weighted a little to help its way
From whence it came. It went back.

The writing, we hope they were
 Reading, expressed a Biblical truth.
'Faith is the substance hoped for,
Evidence of things not seen.'

30. Lay Preacher's Opportunity

Ascending steps, he gained new height.
Now viewing congregation.
So too, his pulpit perorations
Gained gradual momentum.
For those who heard, excitement
Too was raised.
The final thrust of argument
Carried him along, regardless
Of all niceties of grammar.
'Be not afraid', rang through
The ancient arches.
'Hit is I!' Or should that be 'eye'?

(John 6:19-21 KJV)

31. Come to Krasnoyarsk

Siberia, they said, could be very cold.
It proved not so to be.
Precipitation fell as rain, not snow.
Consternation was widespread.

The hotel was of cold-war age,
Where conversations ran along
Wooden conduits and corridors
Heard by those who needed to know.

Everywhere we went, we could not
Avoid them. On landing, lifts,
Down passageways, in foyers,
Dinning hall and doorways.

Singly, or in pairs and threes,
They stretched and pulled
And generally worked all the
Muscles they could find.

There was little room to squeeze
Past these powerful specimens
Of human development as,
Relentlessly, they pumped their iron.

Unfortunate for us, but maybe
Fortunate for some, our visits
Coincided with the Pan Soviet
Women's Wrestling Championships!

32. Here Lies Lenin

With what eager anticipation we planned
Our Soviet excursion on the Waterways of Tsars.
The Cold War almost gone we thought, with safety
Time was right to see the unseeable,
Deny the undeniable and do the undoable.

Old ways die hard, the warning sounded clear.
So we expected prejudice confirmed in
Unexpected ways. Joining the queue with
Sloth-like speed, we drew nearer the long
Awaited goal to see the stuffed remains.

Guarding the door, with staccato sounds, she
Who has to be obeyed, barked her orders loud.
Hands out of pockets, keep moving, no jokes,
No laughter, solemn and serious is 'the standard'.
So he lay, as he had long since done, just dead.

33. The Day the Fish Came in

Running, they came with bowl and bucket
As the word got out, the fish were in.
Not a frequent occurrence by any means
But locals could tell the day and month.
Waves tossed them high onto the steps
And sand. Fish fought and flapped
In such a frenzy. Silver and white in evening
Light, flashed sparkling, as though
Some devouring orca-sized demon
Was set on destruction of all in their sight.
No need to ask what the supper would be,
For there are limited ways whitebait
Can be served to those in Tywyn tonight.

34. Spring?

Brownish birds, beaks full of bits,
Slip with stealth through stems
Not yet greened with growth.
Someone suggested a Blackbird.

Then I saw another. Brownish? Yes,
With flecks of red. Still a beak
Full of bits, but smaller, into the
Ivy slips. Robin, for me, with confidence.

The light raindrops did not deter
The sleek brown predator that
Skulked behind clumps of green,
Watching all things that moved.

He leapt; he pounced, descending
From a height, wrestling it upon
The ground until it seemed all
Life was gone forever. It was a leaf.

35. His Pride

High on the wall his crowing stand was cited.
His harem clucked and scratched below.
Territorial you could call it, as invasion showed.

An early exit through side garden door
Was interrupted. Hurrying to work, bicycle
In hand, he landed in a heap as rooster charged.

Regaining feet, forgetting urgency of work,
After that rooster he ran. On catching it, he
Hatched a plan. Wringing its neck would never do.

Holding its head, thrice round his own he swung,
Gathering momentum on the way. Like some athlete
In competition, he let it go and watched it sail.

It hit the wall and with a thump, in a heap below
Landed seeming lifeless. Pushing his cycle up the hill
To work he went. The rooster stirred and settled back.

Come evening, walking down the hill he came.
A royal greeting now rang out as on his stand
The rooster stood and crowed and crowed and crowed.

36. Behold the Man

Standing in the centre, encircled by his friends
To each was put a question, albeit the same one.
Answers illumined my understanding, for though
All saw Him, knew Him and He them, not one
Could replicate his neighbour's thoughts for each
Perspective was unique, for none in another's shoes stood.

If all of artistic bent had been, and this their
Life-class session, again all perspectives would have
Enriched the static subject; none could see
His neighbour's sight as each pair of eyes saw not
What another saw. If all, at some future moment,
Had gathered their accomplishment, enriched we be.

All would bring a slightly differing portrayal to bear.
None contradictory. All complementary. Each
Insight fresh, as no other would quite have seen.
Now should that one have been the Christ, whose
Promise was to be just that…'In the midst of you,'
How enriched we be – without conflict and in unity.

A helpful stance when disagreement overtakes
And we divided stand: to look to Him, not to our
Brothers raise a stare, as if all faults were there.
Mirror-like, exposed to Him, we stand aghast at
What lies within. Seeing what is inside ourselves,
That we know is there, such plain in others' hearts.

He is a friend. I count him such. Encouragement
He is. Suggested of late I might like to try

Living the outside-in and the inside-out. What
Self exposure that would be, for all to gaze on
Aghast. Horrified, I dare to think, would my
Companions be. Yet, where has my consistence been?

Others thus will always see my faults, my
Double-mindedness and several standards too.
This to one, and that to another, seen. Through
The Rock another name now runs. Bruise me,
Cut me, break me, and inside out, I trust, you
Will find His name, in forgiveness, writ large.

37. Words for a Worship Song

No longer do I need to hold
For I am being held.
No longer do I need to cling
For I am being kept.
You Lord, embrace me now.
No cross of wood, but flesh and blood.
Still your love and mercy
Do what I cannot do today.
When I tried holding on
I just came crashing down again.
When I clung on I slipped
And fell. But you Lord hold me tight.
The way was dark
But you are light.
I could not see
But you saw all.
You took me through the deep.
I would have drowned but for you Lord.
Now You are holding me.
We are loving your embrace,
Just being wrapped around.
Eternity the measure of your grace.

38. Good Friday

Friday, for almost all anticipated.
This one birthed, through fog, sunshine.
A lighter step, almost a smile, on faces.
Greening of hedge rows now begun,
But white of blackthorn predominates.
An air of expectation has been birthed.
Then Friday always was a special day,
Since on a hilltop, long ago, one died.
We now know the life released is here.

39. On Being Eighty

Were I to advance another eighty years,
Would there be no hungry left to feed?
No disputation in conflict of war to end?
Lost forever, prejudice to poison people?

Love, the wake you long to leave behind,
Still opposition, anger, violence and rage,
Encounters, in such measure that its
Death is all too apparent in the everyday.

Poverty, the plight of the vast majority,
Still imprisons those whose hope can never
Live because death does its relentless work
So early in their life, leaving endless sorrow.

Before my time, men left the ground.
Machines in flimsiness, blown by the wind.
Now with conquered moon and space,
Computers too, how I wish I could keep up.

Satellites, in orbit stationary, make many
Borders ineffective. Yet in the minds
Of men, still destruction, devastation,
War and want, all sit in prominence.

From obscurity, seeing the Higgs Bosun
Snatched, and universes uncountable brought
Into light, by means undreamed of in the
Days that consumed my ill-gotten youth,

Exponential is the change that children's
Children learn – that which we never knew.
But fear? Could it but die, its needed death
Allowing joy to have its place restored?

A legacy to leave behind? That presumption's
'Step too far' for one, who to the day he dies,
Still has to learn and live the truth that
All is to be found in following after Jesus.

40. Uncomfortable

They say obesity's become the norm.
Those ranks I do not wish to join.
It has its moments of hilarity,
Yet always at another's uncomfortable expense.

Beside me on the upholstered bench
Type seat, she lowered her frame.
Of proportions ample, it quiveringly
Came to rest, at her uncomfortable expense.

Son or husband, difficult to tell,
Each of equal amplitude, left the
Scene to gather up the Carvery,
To replenish her, at uncomfortable expense.

It was then the noise began,
Setting me wondering whence it came.
Wind was broken, both above and below,
As again she settled, at uncomfortable expense.

'Please dear, do stop it, not in here.
Have some of my acidic drink. That
Always seems to help with you.' Her plate
Piled high, more added to uncomfortable expense.

Between the mastication, jaws in
Perpetual motion, the reverberation
Of the wind could not be stilled, struggling
To get outside, more food for uncomfortable expense.

41. White

Bowing low,
Looking snow-laden,
The branches of the cherry tree.
Blossom, unrestrained, cascades down.
If all bear fruit, the tree will no longer stand.

42. Peace

Two blackbirds can't agree.
Not with each other, I haste to add,
But with the two adjacent nesting jays.
Who got there first might be in dispute.
Comparative size be also in contention.
It could be envy of bright plumage,
But surely not the colour of a beak?
In furious flight, who's chasing whom
Is difficult to determine and who
Is victor when the four sit still?
Just as suddenly, the garden peace
Restored to equilibrium – by a cat.

(Dedicated to all at VNC with gratitude for the Bird Table marking my 80th.)

43. Weekend Approaches

Eyes heavy, but what makes them so?
Stiff joints, but what makes them so?
Not yet four hours free from bed,
And still the clock marks time with ticks.
Within the voice and spirit, in cry, unite:
'Back to the bed with its warmth and
Horizontal posture.' Yet it's only
Ten o'clock on Friday's morn and much to do
Before the day is through…no excuses needed.

44. Egrets at Eastcote

His poise said plurality but I saw only one.
Such is the season – breeding, that is.
That aloneness another story would tell
Of the young male fraternity bent on a mate.

Unwelcome at Blyth Water, solace he sought.
By a stream adjacent the motorway, where
Sounds familiar from Kingsbury gave some
Comfort, there he seemed not distressed.

We liked common sight, standing at bovine
Heels, awaiting disturbance of grub or worm.
He did not see me, though I stopped. Intent
On preening, head tucked away, task assigned.

I'll look for him, though not he for me, the
Next time to Eastcote we tend, to sample
Tea, cake or toast (that will be brown),
And maybe buy the 'climber' I have seen.

Another thought, tangential, this mind pursues.
Around the season the gathering of the males,
Who some say must wait for maturity to start
The ritual pairing before nest is built, begins.

45. View From My Window

Elegantly dressed, his stance exuded only poise.
Early his tailor, knowing black was the new black, quickly
Ran out of the material which left only brown for his bride.
It was the touch of yellow that set the suit to perfection.

His ability to hear the slightest sound astonished
All competitors, as his head, with just the slightest
Tilt, revealed a new angle on his elegance, with
Complemented skill recording vibrations through his feet.

With motion so fast the eye scarcely saw, below
Grass and ground, that yellow weapon thrust. Its
Sharp shaft, with deadly skill and surgical precision
About the task, of accuracy and urgency, to feed a family.

With feet placed the optimum distance apart, leaning
Back, with all his strength exerted, he began to pull.
Hauled, without the clumsiness of breaking as our skill
Would, a whole worm was quickly from its snug grave
snatched.

Devoured, no doubt to be regurgitated later to feed
A growing brood of babes, off he flies in graceful glides
That have direction and purposefulness, declaiming their
 Intent to take him to his predetermined destination.

Then to the height, and on the slenderest branch where
We humans could not stand, he begins his aria. Solo,
 recitative…
Chorus, compliments of two adjacent Robins…begins the

Song exquisite that he has not learned in the avian academy.

With all his elegance and attributes, should not such a
One display ambition? He has no desire to dominate,
Only to keep at bay those who would invade his space.
Content 'par excellence '; relaxed beyond our imagining.

Earlier he has scavenged borders, hedges, and highways
Collecting dross. Collecting what others have, in abundance,
Discarded, cast aside, abandoned. To create, from ashes,
Beauty for his bride to lay her eggs and raise her young.
When talking of relationships, he is a loyal mate and sets
Out in style to captivate his bride; companionship
Creates, with intention that it shall be for life, unlike
Some others of his species which live in adjacent habitat.

Without deceit or jealousy, this gentleman, who makes
My garden 'home', raises family without pretence.
Goes by the humblest of names that left such limited
Impression on those before, who simply called him, Black
Bird.

46. Home

I heard the silence of the sea.
There was no sleep.
I saw the rage and heard the waves.
No to venturing to deep.
Home is where the lullaby is sea.

47. Courtship

Behind the door he kept the gun.
In a relaxed moment following the funeral
It was as though she wanted to let her
Long pent-up feelings find expression.
Oh, she was sad he died but they had
Not been close for years. Separated
Was the word others used, but not herself.

He, from another district came, by name
Of Rocky Point. It was a journey made
On foot in those far-off days, she felt a
Growing need to say. What he had seen
He liked, and there was mutuality abroad.
Alas, her father never would agree. 'If he
Comes again you well know what is behind the door.'

48. University Hospital Coventry

The Atrium has height and light and space.
It also is alive with life,
This opulent entrance to universal health.

Ecologically decorated with its hews of green,
Grey, black and blue.
It almost catches you unaware, a forest clearing.

Through it, you can run, walk or be pushed,
Ride, cavort or be carried,
Or in prone position, be transported.

Retail therapy is catered for, with shops
Placed for those in need,
Alongside the dispensing chemist's alchemy.

If hunger is a problem, two outlets beckon you.
The pretentious coffee shop,
Contending with the style and size of restaurant, no less.

Outside, the helicopter waits to land or lift
Off, carrying the body-parts
Cosseted in their boxes awaiting transplantation.

Central to all surrounding supportive notices
Stands the needed desk,
Manned by volunteers elite who 'all information' know.

The whole spectrum of emotions pass this place. Joy of new life.

Despair, impending death.
Hope that clings to straw and can also last forever.

Here you can breath a sigh, or catch a call or
Even send a text. Yet
Most feared of all, hungry car park 'paying' points.

Revolving, valve-like, the great doors allow for
Simultaneous entrance and exit,
Save when some clot coagulates this artery of life.

What inspiration for design captured architect's
Imagination when hospital
'Brand new' was mentioned – the atrium of heart?

49. Cogitation

Pain, I'm told, is an unpleasant mental
Or physical sensation.
Suffering, I'm told, is to experience such.
Positive pain is the frontline defence
Mechanism of the body.
Continued suffering paves a pathway
Leading to decay and death.
It seems that pain was programmed in Creation
But not the consequential death.
Understanding this, or to use another phrase,
To get one's head around it,
Has taxed the greatest minds and no simplicity
Of answers form a queue.
Banishing pain, and thereby alleviating suffering,
Captures the Hippocratic Oath,
Giving so much respite to a broken world.
Separation in my thinking
Helps my contemplation concerning
Death, coming through disobedience, and Life
Eternal, down death's same road.

50. Taking the Test

The sun is behind you.
The future before you.
No shadows of the coming days
Can darken your today.
Live in the brightness of the moment.
Walk in the light of all your yesterdays.

(Dedicated to Beth McNeil)

51. A Problem Solved

At light's first dawn, he gathered up the tethers
Hanging beside the shed's door, drew back the bolt
And ventured in among the goats.

In semi-darkness he fumbled for the collars,
Securing to each a selected lead, until all were
Now captive to his leadership.

Down the long garden path, where pineapples
Marked the way, he led them to the wasteland
Where they spent each day.

To the tall trees trunks the string and rope was
Tied, so for each goat there was a base from which
He might not roam too far.

Thence, over time, the scrub was cleared as well
As more meat made by those voracious feeders
Eating all in sight each day.

Come end of day, the process was reversed. All
Tethered stock untied and back, up to their nightly
Confine, they were led.

Except on this one day, a quandary confronted the
Goat Keeper. One from his flock, close to his tree trunk,
Had no option left but to sit.

With head bowed down, he ate his way, circumnavigating
The confining mast, in circles of decreasing dimensions,

Until no lead was left.

Looking on, I saw the solution slowly unfolding before
My eyes. With determination in each step, towards the
Erring animal he strode.

Bending down, he picked him up. Secure in his strong arms,
Retraced the steps his captive unwittingly walked to wind
Himself around the tree.

52. My Eye Caught His Picture

He lay as though he fell.
And well he might have done.
All that was covering his
Emaciated form was rags.
When did he last eat?
Food, I mean, not scraps.
Only he would know.
Others would not notice
And least of all not care,
For his companions shared
His same predicament.

There is the difference
Between him and me.
On different continents
Conceived and born,
A vastness of separation
Both in distance and degree.
Not of great wealth
Among my contemporaries
But, compared with him,
Having access to all I need
In food and health and friends.

Will that day come, Lord,
When you will ask me what I did?
You say I saw and was that all?
There was a day, if my
Remembering's right,
A lesson I was taught

By some who were wise
And all grown up and
Thought they knew these things,
That it could well have been you
Lying there. I need to look again.

53. Swallows

Fluttering first caught my eye,
Followed by incessant twittering.
Gaze was upwards drawn.
Memories of childhood stirred.
There upon the wires
They, for a moment, stood.
This way and that, they darted.
Anticipating departure.

Were I sub-Sahara bound,
Preparations prolific would ensue.
They, for the flight,
Scant thought gave,
And how did they know the way?
To a pilot I would trust my lot.
Would his navigation skills
Match theirs?

My time in hours
Would measured be,
Whilst theirs in days be numbered.
I, in cosseted comfort.
They, to the elements exposed.
With excess baggage paid,
Yet they without a care, traversed
The same terrain.

54. Pic and Mix

He saw it on the counters.
He saw it on TV.
Children asked for pennies
To buy what they could see.

Sweets displayed
With choice and taste.
Bulbs for the borders, spring.
Birthing a Pic and Mix in him.

Early to the surgery,
Before the patients came,
All the samples he'd received
Filled up a box without a name.

'Help Yourself' the
Notice read, displayed
For all to see. Please Pic
And Mix, just don't trouble me.

When next the GMC
Convened, to hear all that might be.
Complaints were such, no blind eye
Was turned to mitigate his plea.

No Pic and Mix prescriptions
Could be considered free.
His name, alas, could not be deemed
Upon their list to be.

(Reflections on a report in a certain newspaper)

55. Reflections

My time has been. It's come and gone. Others must be the
    judge.
Did I set out to change the world? No such grandiose
    pretensions.
What motivated mechanic to minister, is contained within a
    'call'.
Some will laugh, some might cry, but self-examination might,
    just
Might, discover you too, in your own way ran after a 'call' of
    sorts.

Yours is to assail a different world from that which I passed
    through.
There is no streak of envy in this tired frame. Just a passing
    thought.
Did parents perhaps think, before the procreation act, of the
    world
You might be entering? Darkest clouds of war hung heavy
    over
The shadows of brooks that bisected the Cotswold Vale of
    Bourton.

Light came, but then more darkness caressed the horizons
    both of
Mind and hills. Where your going will take you, I cannot
    foretell.
The only certainty is that day will often seem as night.
Atrocity
Upon atrocity will drive compassion far away, until it seems
    as though

Hope and light and joy and peace, all once held dear, are gone.

Has the optimist become confirmed in eternal pessimism? Maybe.
But when your time comes for copulation to ensue in procreation,
Pause to think. Choices are yours, denied the many of former times.
The dead, sometimes called blessed, may have the better part.
Long they have left the fearful future and see not what was behind.

'A Brave New World' has yet more brave to be. Will your children,
And their children's children, thank you for the gift of life you gave?
There is a positive assertion that says they will. Yet, how will they
Find preparation when catapulted into chaos all too soon, lacking
Wisdom, maturity, understanding, relationship, stability and joy?

Forefathers, fearful of the future, in every generation were there.
Never a time when doom-mongers were not. No extinction experienced.
Control, conformity and power strangles each succeeding generation.
As the world becomes a smaller place and as the mind of man ceases

To engage his brain, hope - before its birth - is terminated in death.

To live through days and decades, through months and millennia,
Into the future's far-distant landscapes, will be to see new generations
Of the brave, the noble and the just rise to face the challenges
That lie ahead. It can be spelt as hope, or confidence. A resounding 'Yes'
Says that your children's children will be there, out in front.

56. Seeing Leaves in Autumn

Whose hand, the golden weft and warp
Of autumn leaves, patterned perfection
Beneath the beech and sycamore?

Whose eyes discerned that green could
Fade and, in its death throes, release
A spectrum - rainbow in perfection?

Whose thought, with you and me in mind,
Released white light to be shattered in
The prism, from invisibility to what we see?

Gratitude is mine, to give as generously
As I received, with sight and sound and
Touch and smell, not excluding taste as well.

57. Street Scene

It stood, drawn vertically by strong sun's rays capturing the light,
To give it leaf and life, but now seemed dark, brittle, brown and dead.
We walked upon that the eye could not see, buried beneath pavement,
And knew that, there, some life lurked named the sap, waiting to rise.

People passed by, giving not a glimpse at the unmoving bear branches.
Were they too in winter's grasp as, bowed, they bent against the cold?
Was sap secreted in the soul, waiting for the warmth of Spring to rise?
An optimistic streak in me said 'Yes' to both the tree and human traffic.

58. Solihull Café Rouge

Maroon and cream of High Street spells out the Cafe Rougé,
With chairs and tables pavement mounted, set there each morn.
Step inside to spotted script, awaiting antibiotic's latest strain,
And contorted thorns with roses set among the pseudo art:
La Framboisette, au la vin blanc, au vermouth, au champagne,
Au l'eau de seltz, awaiting the departing train among the many
Hanging adverts of out-dated exhibitions; bevel-edged mirrors
Scattering prismatic light in many colours, midst the cheeky
Pictures of a bygone Paris captured in a host of coloured cartoon.

Decor is not the invitation drawing you to venture further in.
Rather the red menus which, in immaculate French, detail
The delights of Le Petit **Déjeuner**, Hors D'oeuvres, Salades,
Plats Principaux, and Sides. Some steaks too. A Taste of France.
Vin of course is there but, depending on the time of day, it
May well be Latte, Cappuccino, **Espresso** of your choice, to
Lubricate the larynx or loosen the lungs - stimulate the brain.
Then meet the backbone of every outlet, those amazing staff.
Cook to waiter, manager to barista, from all the nations named.

Français their language may not be but, here and there, phrases
Fall that belie the effort made for every connoisseur of fine

Food, to feel they may be, for one moment, on the banks of Seine.
Hungary, Romania, Poland, Czech Republic and the misplaced French,
Along with many others, go to make up that provocation which
Says 'I will return and sample once again this delightful cuisine.'
Yet when the time to pay the check arrives, more incentives to
Return are found, for be it he or she, it matters not, the offers
Are the same. Come again, the 'two for one' and 'forty percent off'.

59. Shadowbrook Buzzards

        Shadowbrook.
        Today I saw them.
        The stately silhouettes
       Darkest against the azure blue
      No beat of wing to hurry silent glide.
      Masters of effortless movement
       Whose shape is changed
      By each twist or turn.
     Buzzards.

Heavenward
  A young child's piercing
    Cry is heard. But for those
      Who know, it is the buzzard's retort, when,
       Being mobbed by other birds who do not
        Wish it well.
          Chasing, climbing, diving they pursue as
          Foe. This raptor cruising the sky.
           Lazily he moves carefree.
           Languidly.

        Suddenly,
        The darkest shadow
       Moved before the vehicle.
     Vast black wavering wings sweeping
    The broad driveway before the haunting
   Greyness of the Manor, leavings it's
  Guardian fence post where
Watching for prey. Dispatched.

60. Creed?

A Creed to hold me to account or stress my orthodoxy?
To say thus I believe, now count yourself a heretic.
There was a day when match was stuck to test your veracity.
Write it down and, having writ, never, ever move on.

But when that creed has essence in a person that allows
Not the written form, what then for orthodoxy's measure?
Writhe and wriggle with duplicity, your words spell failure,
For their purpose was not meant to confine life of the divine.

My creed has eyes of blue or brown, hair to be styled and
Beard to be grown. Hands to work and feet to run, a heart's
Passion experienced in, and **through** love, kindness,
    forgiveness.
Captured in compassion, blended with perfection of
    acceptance.

61. Shalome

We have not held you in our hands,
Only in my womb. Your fragile life
Received as gift to carry to full term;
Seen only with the scan's ability
To hide me and reveal your all.
Close to our hearts in love, in thought,
In prayer, yet nearer the beating
Rhythm where affinity was born.
Though separation is the goal,
It never can take place, for we
Who, joined as one, have a secret
Place where peace is birthed through
Faith – flooding all dark remembered days.

(Dedicated to E J and Colin)

62. 'When You Come Together'

Across the blue expanse of sky,
The radiance of the golden sun
Cascades in glory's brightness.

I carried this as I came inside
To engage the head, the heart,
The mind and spirit's worship.

He met me as, low to lower, I
Was brought by splendour of
His nearest presence. Oh, so close.

Consuming, burning, purifying,
All that, with His Being there, could
Not co-exist. Gone. I felt so clean.

Was this the purpose of His choice?
I do not know, or have a care, for
In that moment I was born anew.

You were there too and somehow,
Now the two of us are, as one, along
With all the others, congregating.

63. Going Home

If this day of departure was but the moment of arrival,
What emotions might I now experience,
Could that be but changed.
Leaving for arrival, at a moment of will, could change all.

Yet, is that not the way it sometimes falls?
The unexpected for the familiar,
Exceptional for ordinary, interposed.
Here to linger and to dream, maybe some day.

Yet, it is only in the moment that I am
On ground that is uncertain: having nothing
Of security known. So, where is home
When needed, from which I was so eager to escape?

64. Did the Supreme Court get it Right?

Of late, I found reflection upon hate
Confusing, troubling, offensive and painful.
Where might it have been born and raised?
Of certainty, it is a prolific breeder.

I heard that the food of hate is fear.
'Whom shall I fear, of whom shall I be afraid?'
Can be quoted from a heart holding hate
And giving expression to a lie within.

To 'hate the sin and love the sinner'
Is a pious platitude that drips from mealy
Mouths that bring a doubled mindedness,
Making excuse to validate the indefensible.

I was told that love perfect casts out fear.
Fool that I am, I believe this to be true.
So, too, I believe that my God is love and, if that
Be true, He can have no segment labelled 'Hate'.

So now I have to pause and think again.
To be called His daughter or His son has to
Preclude hate from my repertoire of response.
In his all encompassing love, hate cannot co-exist.

I refuse to return hate for hate. I will not
Be told to hate you for whatever cause you
Might hate me. Be it faith, ethnicity or gender,
Or ought else. I will try to reflect His love to you.

For, be that love perfection, it cannot
Hold within its circumference ought that be
Of fear or hate. To do so would be to deny
Itself, destroy itself, and be no longer God.

65. Wedding Interruption

The Wedding began as he made his way in.
Joining the groom's side, with strange looking grin,
Pushing past ushers, with mumblings of sin.
Blood, the first to be caught by the eye.
Then nose coming next, detecting a dye.
Disheveled appearance, apparel not suited

Wondering who mistook him for guest?
To whom would invitations be sent next?
For such moments as these, long
Since I'd prepared. High street location
Gave rise to surprise which, at the
Right time, some favour might find.

Interruptions, inappropriate, came to my
Mind. With steady step, my bouncers
Arrived. Sidestepping in pews, 'til,
One on each side, they lifted him up,
At the elbows no less, as his feet fought
For footing and could find not one.

He was moved from the pew, to the aisle,
Through the lobby, down steps, then
Standing outside, a look of surprise came
Over his face, as never, no never, such fast
Exit from church had he found. They were
Waiting, surprised, the bold men in Blue.

66. Black and White or White

Our car pulled up close to the pavement edge.
Three were black and one was white. The town
Was Britts, South Africa. Apartheid here was
Not yet dead for this was home to white
Supremacy. The territory of Terrance Blanche.

To say all eyes were turned upon us
Would in no way overstate the case
It seemed as if even horses and dogs
Turned their eyes on us in disapproval.
Never had hair on my neck reacted like this.

Business at the bank done, car was filled again
Beating a hasty departure all were pleased
To be right out of that town. It seemed
That had we not, we might be driven out.
Three black, one white clearly not approved.

Three black, one white another time
Another place. A roadside puncture repair
Station, in the township of our stay.
Jack in place, car lifted high, wheel off
In no time at all. accomplished efficiently.

Another car pulled up. No puncture apparent.
Occupants both white, a young man and his bride,
Judging by the vehicles decoration.
The male got out, visibly shaking from
Head to toe. Fear gripped his face.

Trembling, he made straight for me.
With quivering voice exclaiming, 'We are
Lost. I took a wrong turn and ended up
Among the blacks.' 'What are you doing here,
Aren't you afraid, you could be robbed or worse.'

So I'm his white salvation, or so he thought.
'What can I do', I asked him. 'Tell us the way',
He blurted out. 'Get us out of here, quick'.
'I'am a stranger too. My friends may know the way'.
She was crouched down low not wanting to be seen.

'You talk to them, they're black,' was his reply.
He tried to stand as far from them as possible.
'Ask them yourself, they will not bite'. I loudly said,
'I can't ask. I don't know where you want to go
And as I don't know where I am, what is the point.

He had to talk to them, they with politeness,
Of which he had none. His voice betrayed his
Fear as one of the others walked towards his car.
Carefully they explained to him the way that he
Should take to find their safety and destination.
Never did we dream that life could be so divided.
He ran back to his bride, started the engine of the car
And accelerated away, as though the lights were
Out and the race had started. 'What was that about',
I said. 'Why should they be afraid of friends who help?'

67. Mysterious Fruit

Way down in the deep recesses of the mind
That name rested, waiting an unlikely call from
Its darkness, to a consciousness of significance.

When the call came , like many another words
Lost to minds ability to resurrect, nothing was
Forthcoming. More forgetfulness coming with age.

So I picked one, rolling it in my hand to jog my
Mind, still nothing stirred, no recognition, no
Ideas flickered round the brain finding the mouth.

Google, of course would do it, save for one intractable
Problem. What word to type to set the search engines
In motion finding millions in a matter of moments.

Finally I put it in his hands, scared and gnarled,
With time in nature and garden labour. Brighter
Than computerised power, 'That be a Medlar, Son.'

68. Orlando

What did the native American Indians feel
When those white Christians came and stole
Everything they had, even the ground upon
Which they stood?

And likewise the original inhabitants of
The antipodes overrun by criminal and carer,
To the extent that even written rocks
Were deemed dead?

What too of the world we went plundering;
Remembered on a day of indoctrination
At school as Empire Day was celebrated?
We all stood still.

Looking for humility today, whence and
Where upon the landscape of the nations,
Echoing around a wounded world of people,
Can it be found?

To recognise this planet Earth belongs to
Each and everyone, born to breath its common
Air and the share the brightness of the glorious sun,
Made for all mankind?

Everyday humility and love are killed. Too slow
The Cross, bullets do the same, but quicker.
Therefore more can be mown down in given time.
Hate again walks tall.

He lived, counting others better than Himself,
Encouraged us not to think too highly of ourselves,
To be found as those preferring others, as He did..
All of that for me.

69. Today a Memory Lingers

Forty six years ago
A boy was born to bear the name of Andrew.
In his short life he learned to live, to love,
To work, to serve and bring joy with blessing.
Son not just today but everyday your name is called.

(Mum and Dad)

70. Elusive Sleep

Now it is night, the essence of the day,
When all that I have done becomes distilled
Into the tangled thoughts that now embrace
Tomorrow with which I have yet to deal.

Night, when the reality of day becomes
Entangled with the new reality of dream.
Here is the life that might have been,
That could have been, were I not wide awake.

Holding excitement of anticipated embrace,
It does nought to satisfy the senses save
Create havoc among the lurking hormones
And irony of ironies I woke remembering nought.

71. Referendum

Passing words, a lingering phrase,
Hung in my mind and round its
Circumnavigation of my head
Looking for meaning, orbited.

Restless, it found no place to
Linger, nothing to detain the
Motion. Thus begun, it continued
On, making no sense or reason.

Does that both begin and end?
Liquids flow, as too ideas, finding
Natural levels becoming stationary
Until moved on by some new motion.

'That which flows from this', I
Heard him. A question could invoke,
Causing contemplation to give added
Momentum to a muddled mind.

Revolutions. as in revolving, onward
Goes the mind, in thinking thoughts
It might not otherwise have done,
Had someone not said cast a vote.

72. Time Change

In 1559 or there abouts, a building was began.
Willow, mud, water and buckets to hand,
The wattle and daub brigade arrived to bolster
Stone masons, carpenters and labourers
Bent on building the new dwelling to add adornment
To the well established town of Solihull,
Creating that which they knew not would still be
Inhabited almost five hundred years hence.
Still to this day you can view their handiwork,
Through the glass panel set in modern
Stone of generations later, refurbishment exposed.
Now a High Street Tavern serving fine
French Cuisine under the name of Café Rouge.

73. Advent's Coming Freedom

The word was out. Behind the hand. Have you heard?,
'She's pregnant'. Who's the father then? By God both will
Be in trouble. I would not like to be in their shoes.

But she, 'by God, that's right'. You never will believe it.
Joseph said t'was nought to do with him and if by God
There would be some accounting to be done at home.

Not a great beginning for salvation, restoration, renewal
And resurrection. The babe, the boy, teenager and the
Stirrer up of trouble. Only one way out then, crucifixion.

Lazarus was four days dead when Jesus called him out.
This boy would be but three before the stone was rolled away.
Stumbling out into the light they tore his blindfold off.

Standing there he saw his friend, then came embrace.
By God, that's advent and a half if you hear Him call your
    name.
This Christmas time you too can be set free, by God.

74. Confidence

I did not fall, just overcome and lay down to rest.
His arms were strong to raise me up. Looking kind,
The dust he brushed away, smiles broke across
A countenance that said, your welcome, peace.

No interrogation captured me. What great relief.
It all spilled out, myself as I saw me, ashamed
In such a presence that had me disclose more
Than I would dare tell you or even tell myself.

What was that? I'm sure I felt a tighter grip,
But still a gentle hold. No condemnation when
It was so well deserved. Compassion, acceptance,
Love all crowd around and cloak a form in pain.

Nowhere, in the wideness of experience, can
Such intensity of love find a place to rest.
Striving stops. Anxiety melts. Fear is forgotten.
Who you are is found only in He who holds.

75. Advent Reflections

Future is a place I do not know.
The past has been my habitation.
Future is a place of anticipation.
The past gathering only regrets.

I was asked to reflect on Advent.
Anticipating death seems futures
Reality stimulating a longing for the
Nostalgia of times long since gone by.

An arrival, it is said. A coming too.
A first and second, so I have heard.
Reflecting stirs both a pleasure
And a pain. My mortal destiny for sure.

Then again it is not about me but Him.
The one who both came and is coming.
Taking futures fear away restoring
Confidence that I might live in Him.

76. Abstract Pain

Abstract pain sets hares a running.
Panic drives the brain.
Middle chest and breathlessness provokes a 999.
It moves, thank God and I can rest my anxious mind.
But no. There it is again.
The maddening world revolves once more.
Horizontal posture is he the only one.
A dream? To wake would be pure delight
But for the abstract pain setting me off again.

77. I Planted Him

Now standing almost forty feet, outlined
Against a leaden sky, the pine tree gently
Sways as breeze moves across the fence.

There was a day I held him in my hand. The
Seed, I mean, but then not one but three.
Germination over, I chose the stronger.

On the window sill he began to grow tiny
Green needles which long since have gone.
The far border became his place of maturing.

Twenty years have passed and now its
Towering hight dominates the garden.
Branches trimmed to yield logs to burn.

Have my passing years of growth yielded as
Much to be admired as his great stateliness?
I fear not, nor been pruned as he has been.

Were I such a thing of beauty and of stature
Bending to the wild winds torturous turns
I think I would long since have succumbed.

My fate could well have been cremated fire logs
Enhancing with heat some neighbours grate.
Alas, I do not want to be a tree for all its loftiness.

However, in these days of ecological concerns
Where six foot under would be the norm unless

There are two, then cremation could well be fate.

78. Past Christmas Recalled

The day dawns and it Christmas morn.
No longer children given to early rise
A more leisurely start to the day is
Marked for those of more maturing years.

Nevertheless, the memory can still recall
Those moments in the night, or so our
Parents would have called them, that
Marked the beginning of the magical morn.

Creeping quietly down the ill lit stairs so
As not to wake the households other guests,
Or for that matter competing siblings.
Get there first and you might win a prize.

Your largest pair of socks were hung the
Night before from the tall Mantel Piece.
But with a warning this year I remember.
'Not this time with war on, we have nothing.'

War would not put us off even if parents
Were thinking otherwise. So time for the
Same routine to be followed. Descent began.
All the house awoke to the cry, 'Its empty'.

'We told you not to hang them up this year',
Was not a consolation children could take in.
It was a Christmas morn to be remembered.
Haunting the memory down the years, a lesson.

How many will be the children damaged by
Wars around the world today? Doomed to
Distress and disappointment as a life style
Countless they will be. Do we hear their cry?

That experience began to forge a lifestyle
Which declared an intention to banish every
Disappointment wherever that would be a
Possibility, so if I ever let you down, please forgive.

79. Another Year

But when all is said and done it is only a means
Of counting, enabling a journey into the past or
Into the future to be hashtaged in time.
The very existence of which owes its origins to
Man's creation, as opposed to matter or its anti.

Understanding integration in universal theories
Has occupied and still does occupy, the greatest
Minds that humankind can bring to bear upon the
Fascination of our existence, as from whence we
Came and whither we are headlong bound, before

Another year is born and the inevitable speculation
Begins in earnest. Her New Year Message and his
Welcome to the next twelve months, set markers
Down that otherwise may not have been created to
The chagrin of the masses and their entourage.

Welcome then to the bride of our existence. To
See you means that the life support has not yet
Been turned off as some might have supposed.
As to an appropriate introduction I am not a
Little confused. But here you are, lets get on.

80. Outlook

Middle England has become their home.
The land. to them, more familiar than the sea.
There was a time, when to hear their call,
You took a charabanc on a Sunday School
Outing, a Weston or a Bournemouth destination.
With raucous call they cleaved the sky and
Stole the unsuspecting food of chip or ice cream,
Dependant on starter, main or dessert.

White against the leaden sky or grey against
The blue depending on the sun's visibility,
They sweep majestic, pealing left or right
Looking for what is invisible to us. Pausing
To rest a while upon the provision of the
Well positioned lamp post with extending arm
Across the footpath thirty feet below, they
Shuffle, finding room for seven on each.

Gathered in a group of twenty one, or three
Lamp posts, if you want to be precise, they
Patrol the park, scouring the grass for what?
A lonesome dog divides them into two uneven
Groups and somehow they are not happy.
Lifting off they fast return to the numerical
Equilibrium of lamp posts, there awaiting a
Signal that eludes my inquisitiveness.

I might have fared better with maths when
Attending Grammar School had these pesky
Birds migrated inland sooner. But then again

The view from bedroom window was barred
By five mighty elms that dwarfed all other
Arboreal manifestation. Soon they succumbed
To fellers axe and crosscuts, gone for good.
Later, to complete the task came Dutch Elm.

That disease annihilated elm, even when hidden
In the hedgerow as tender saplings seeking
Anonymity. The flaying wings engaged attention
In a different place as almost all of twenty one
Gathered on a long fallen elm trunk left for those
Invading the public space to play, pretend and climb.
Almost, I say, as I let my gaze return to the street
Illumination, for there were four, leaving seventeen?

81. Just Thinking

The dipping earth delivers dawn and the same rotation
Heralds the approaching darkness through the dusk.
One continuous motion creating opposite and apposite.
Darkness giving way to light and light's fate a darkness
Of the night.

And in that contradictory continuum we have been set.
Learning to create both light and darkness, to extend
These two colossi of a constellation, speaks dissatisfaction.
If that could be used to describe the urge of investigation
Not of rest.

Another avenue of thought pursues more of the same.
War and peace have their progenitors prolonging one
At the expense of the other. Yet life and death puzzle
The engaging mind. Opportunity collides with extinction.
So no more.

82. Tears

I am told there are two mechanisms working when tears flow.
The biological consequence that cause tear duct secretion.
Then what stabbed the heart that wrenched the emotion that
Preceded the warm sensation of soft wetness on the cheeks.

As to the former, you can, by learning, discover bodies' secrets.
As to the later, the physiological GPS has no value helping to
Unfold the stories that, in a second, explode in magnitude
Scattering an avalanche of memories into a storm of moments.

For each of them one small tear rolling inexorably down the
Steepness of the soft cheek recounting love, joy, excitement.
Fear and trust, held in an embrace separated only by the minds
Inability to recall everything that passed before. Now hope.

Wet eyes are gently patted. Tissues need regular renewal.
Inside a life is throbbing to emotions beat. To hold and be held
Gives warmth, shares an ache and speaks not in words but
Syllables of sobs which the heart was made to understand.

83. Time to Update

Silently, in sparkling beauty, effortlessly
Across the shimmering sunlit garden space,
Bearing beneath them a precious cargo,
Life, packaged in the smallest of seeds,
Of old, delightful description, thistle down.
Now in modernity, natures own delivery drone.

84. Fulfilment not Postponement

'It is finished', echoed through the universe from
An obscure hilltop, named Calvary. And from a cross
He proclaimed a Kingdom, not of this world. Present
And yet awaiting consummation in an age to come,
Immutable, abiding, birthed through His broken body.

Completed, the assignment given by the Father
And the Spirit in the courts of their domicile.
Redemption, reconciliation, restoration, reunion,
Love wins though. Humiliation, hatred, hostility and
Death itself have met their match in life laid down.

One who followed gave more expression when he
Began a peroration. No longer Jew or Gentile,
Slave or free, female and male, circumcised or
Uncircumcised, barbarian, Scythian. Today the list
Continues adding straight and gay, black or white.

State and nationhood are found there too. So claim
Your homeland distinction, your differentiating,
Distinguishing facts, features, origin, ancestry,
Genetic pool or even mitochondria dna. All, yes all,
One in Him. Nothing now can separate…

Is there a price? Yes, it is paid. Is there ought that
I must do to find my place in paradise beside that
Triune majesty in elysian rest at the great culmination?
Yes again, but this time only you can say the word,
Confess with heart, breathe the sigh that says, 'I'm in'.

85. An Inadvertent Glance

Rain began to fall, heads began to bow, shoulders hunched.
The pavement limited the view as strides were checked.
It seemed almost a reluctant glance, but I looked up. It
Shone, the moon, its brightness captured my attention.
From here to there someone has gone and placed his feet
As firmly as mine now stand upon these paving stones.
A dream. a jump. Could prehistoric man have conceived
In his wildest imaginings that one day his descendants
Would look back and see from where I now stood, thinking?

Projecting forward, as minds have habits of so doing,
I thought myself as now most primitive. Looking forward,
What might ten or twenty generations from this time
Be smiling as they too look back. In my pocket I have a
Device that could tell me where in all the world I might
Be standing in this very moment. GPS comes to mind, I
Might be wrong. However, I believe that my descendants
Could press one button and in but a fraction of a moment
Be standing there, transmogrified. I looked up and saw.

86. Our Feasts

With excitement and encouragement, our Book reveals God's
Will for us to celebrate and play, remembering past, rejoicing
   now,
Whilst setting down the markers for the days and years to
   come.
Feasts, festivals, festivities, commemorations, all encircling a
   year
Marking for us and for our offspring the cycle of His
   faithfulness,
Reflecting holiness, forgiveness, endurance, peace and love.

So I thought to look, with a tangential eye, and enquired
   within.
I didn't think an apple shared to be much of a feast. But when
You have been watching it long ripen, green to red, shinning
   in
The sunlight, then told you cannot eat, saved for someone
   else
And only Adam's here, what then? He slithered past and said,
"Go on." Then again, that bite inaugurated all succeeding
   feasts.

Only twelve invited. Preparation time was short. He fixed it
With a man to carry a pot upon his head and lead his friends
To the room got ready just in time. "A table with thirteen
   chairs
Should really be enough, then the usual menu for passover.
We'll lock the door and leave you to clear away. I don't count
On staying late as tomorrow is another day going down in
   history."

From memory this cannot be written as it has not happened yet.
All we know there is a groom and He will have a bride whose robes
Will have been especially washed in redness of an apple, blood.
They came out white, whiter than white, and shone with a golden
Glow of dawn. A feast, a spectacle, festivity, in all creation not
To be brought to an end as in the beginning, so now, paradise again.

87. Just a Thought

A moment of eternity flashed though space and time.
Charged with all I'd ever thought or ever dreamed.
But more. In that moment was conception, birth, life
And death. Nothing seemed excluded, nothing extraneous.
Resurrection seemed a climax, the culmination of
This stellar event known in the Bible as God's 'Today'.

His 'Today' of paradise; 'Today' of choice; 'Today' of life.
Reflecting on such it turned thoughts to beginnings,
To ends and in betweens. This moment contained all
That ever has or ever will, excluding nothing that is.
A start seems to imply a before as does an end also.
Located within divinity bearing both a touch and feel.

Some scientists search. Some theologians think.
Contemplations of cessation, accelerates nothing,
Termination is temporal, encompassed as it is in this
Event that does not start, is never finished, nor
Complete, save in the succession of such. Unreal it
All may be. But please tell me this, what is Eternity?.

88. Ask Not of Me...

One hundred years ago my grandad died trying,
Along with many more, to piece it all together
Yet again. But still it fell to father's generation
To try and do the same. What cost success?
Now, for me, eighty three years have passed.
Let no one lie to you. It was not this event,
Momentous as it seems, that triggered Article 50.
A portend of European disintegration and destruction,
Discombobulated, and dumfounded, have we nothing
Learned. To whose great grandchildren
Will it future fall, to lay down lives for pardon,
Peace, and prosperity yet again to prevail?

89. Does it Matter?

Spring has certainly come.
The daffodils are over and done.
The birds have built and chosen a mate.
The farmer's daughter was seen at the gate.
Time again to look for the sun
Before the clouds decide whose won.
The greening of hedgerows and fields has begun.
But the poor old pensioners still look glum.
Pause for a moment and think of the sad.
What's in this season to make anyone glad?

90. What the Dickens?

Not a Tale of two Cities this time.

"It was the best of times, it was the worst of times,
it was the age of wisdom, it was the age of foolishness,
it was the epoch of belief, it was the epoch of incredulity,
it was the season of Light, it was the season of darkness,
it was the spring of hope, it was the winter of despair,
we had everything before us, we had nothing before us,
we were all going direct to Heaven, we were all going direct
the other way."

This time a Tale of two Gardens some said.

An eden, paradise, perfection.
That is until Adam arrived with
A wife, an apple and snake.
A time of contrasts too.
Awake, asleep, fear filled and faithful,
My will and thy will, oh, for heavens sake.
As what was lost is now up to be saved.
Not an Adam but Jesus, Son of man,
Son of God. Nat barred from a garden
But raised to the sky. Not a tree full of life,
But now being dead, fashioned to a cross.

Outcomes, yes, outcomes that's what we must have.
However long it takes.
What's your patience like?
Could it last a day, or two, or maybe three?

91. Thursday Night Through Friday

Washing dirty, smelly feet marks out the man.
Not to be served but to serve, He said. It showed.

A secrecy of plans laid proved to be a great success.
Did He really say bread was flesh and wine was blood?

Long the day, eyes so very tired, they'll not stay open.
What's going to happen? Sweat like drops of blood.

A rough crowd gathers round, then a caress and kiss.
That's right, I told you, now I'm off. Its finished.

Commotion, confusion. A sword is swung. Down falls
An ear. Quickly replaced by gentle touch, healed.

You are who? Since when? Yes, we will remember that!
Take Him down, play with him, then take Him up the hill.

Purple robe and crown of thorns to mock, to scorn.
Blindfold, spin round, who hit you then? Don't know?

Soon be Noon. You got the nails? I'll bring the hammer.
He can carry his own cross. We've already dug the hole.

Lie him down. Give me the hammer, I'll do the feet.
Heave on that rope, up He goes. In the socket first.

Right, now throw the dice, not many bits but spare
The robe. Its woven in one piece. make a good blanket.

You alright up there, we have a drink to dull the pain.
Who you taking to? Yes, You can forgive, but its our job.

He didn't last as long as most, perhaps it was the heat.
Ah well, He'll have to wait 'til the other two are gone.

92. Running with the Wild

The bush was thick, the grass was standing tall.
Then the lair came into view, old termites built.
Reason exposed why it waved without the wind.
Hyenas with purpose moving to gather cubs.

Feeding time. Scavengers abroad write fear in
Every moving thing. They snatch and tear their meat
From the living or the dead to feed the buried cubs
Secure deep underground in litters sheltering.

From Africa's deep South now drawn to its North
Eastern lands. A country called Ethiopia evocative
In every way. Rich in tradition giving history a
New dimension with Axum and the Temple's Ark.

There too these most dreaded beasts patrol.
Here to be encountered at a new exciting level.
'Yes, thats right sir, you may get to feed them.'
Running wild hyenas? Skepticism pulsed in veins.

Fed for years in the surrounding hills of Harar
Keeping at bay those marauding canines from
Livestock and the careless child who strayed.
Slowly they migrated to the cities limiting walls.

Not long detained, those piercing eyes darkness
In streets defied and curdling calls broke
The silence of the night as teeth again tore
Flesh from bone and sinew from its security.

Bravely he threw the scraps of meat and kept
Them corralled at bay. What quirk of minds
Intention made of protection's fear a potential
Of the strangest for tourist attractions here?

Now trembling in darkness, only disturbed by
Vehicles headlights, you wait to hear him call
Them by name. Seeming design disasters they
Lollop along and claim their morsel from the stick.

Through the darkness ten or twenty, maybe more.
He motioned to me, holding out the stick, Forward,
Brushing one along the way, gingerly I made way.
The meat just holding on a shaking cane. Will he?

Trying hard to hold it still, I sat down beside that
Most remarkable of men. One quick gulp, meat
And wild Hyena gone. But not for good. I watched
And he returned for more. Running with the wild.

93. Explosion

Is it not self evident that what we did and do abroad
Should come to rest upon our shores in consequences
Chaotic in nature? Global economy, finance, and trade
Now embrace war, unconfined to boundaries as once
You could go off to. All you need to do now is stay put.
It will assuredly come to you. Time for political rethink?

Still to the future all must look. There the tomorrow's
Truth is clothed in invisibility. All that can be seen has
Come and gone. Likewise the future's voice cannot be
Heard. It has not yet spoken, though some believe it so.
What is to be then, has it roots in what's already been.
Listening, looking, learning, reconfiguring, marks a road.

Have not the wise of every race, creed and culture
Behoved us to handle with great care all that is and
Has been. 'Learn the lessons of the past,' a mantra that
Must not be lost. Unlike the world of science where
All that's there is yet to be discovered. History is
Not for discovering. It is for writing, oft in blood.

The gentlest step, the softest touch, are guides to
Take a forward path where, the cruelty, the hatred,
The bitterness of war, and wholesale destruction of
A nuclear nature, have never told love's simple truth.
Each giving preference to the other, expressing
Compassion's love and tears has still to see reality.

My freedom to write such lines as these offence may
Cause to some, whilst others take for granted licence

Given to me. Intention has a clarity in context here.
Life, and letting all live, as they would perhaps
Willing share with others, on such a tiny planet in the
Swirling mass of cosmological certitude making Earth.

94. Eternity

A moment of Eternity flashes though Space and Time,
Charged with all I'd ever thought or ever dreamed.
But more. In that moment was conception, birth, life
And death. Nothing seemed excluded, nothing extraneous.
Resurrection seemed a climax, the culmination of
This stellar event known in the Bible as God's 'Today'.

His 'Today' of paradise; 'Today' of choice; 'Today' of life.
Reflecting on such it turned thoughts to beginnings,
To ends and in betweens. This moment contained all
That ever has or ever will, excluding nothing that is.
A start seems to imply a before as does an end also.
Located within divinity bearing both a touch and feel.

Some scientists search, some theologians think.
Contemplations of cessation, accelerates nothing,
Termination is temporal, encompassed as it is in this
Event that does not start, is never finished, nor
Complete, save in the succession of such. Unreal it
All may be. But please tell me this, what is Eternity?.

95. Tick Box Innocence

Did my vote allow the rule?
Did my vote approve the Law?
Did my work pay the tax?
Did my hands mine the ore?
Did my hands make the metal?
Did my hands fashion the weapon?
Did my diplomacy sell the weapons?
Did my skills pilot the plane?
Did my hands release the bomb?

No. A thousand times no,
Save for the one small, Yes.
Shall I ever find forgiveness
Where I thought I needed none?

Now terror unleashed has come
So close to home that our windows
Now are shaken, our children dying,
And visitors to our shores killed.

For all political protestations,
Enough is enough and things have
Got to change, did we not in shelters
Hide from bombs the enemy released.

96. Standing at School

Asking when did it really start is a
Question uncomfortable in every respect.
The boomerang of consequence returns
To visit us as we have visited them.

Those who sow the wind have a
Whirlwind to reap and we were they
Who from our shores set forth
To rob and pillage round the world.

Empire, we called it, that is until
The world could stomach it no longer
And Commonwealth became more
Acceptable to most but not to all.

Asking if it be possible to make
Sense of all that passes for progress
In our time, what can be said save
Some be too old, remembering too much

97. Table Top Reflections

It stands upon a pillar, stable with a broadened base.
Give it then two legs, with stability thus compromised
There needs a base as broad, to bear the load above.
When three are given reign, strength abounds in triplicate.
But four seems, by common consent, to be the optimum.

Is this analogous to the business models hammered
Out in prolonged debate upon its shinning surface?
'We need to bring more strength to this enterprise
If we are going to experience growth, and stability',
Has often been heard as wisdom invades the boardroom.

But with a new dimension, length, comes need again.
More legs are brought into play, enabling rigidity.
Then materials of manufacture might be discussed
With plastic, laminate, formica and aluminium brought
To the table, so to speak. Can you really better Oak?

Most common use must be a meal. Some famous ones
Stand out. That painted by Leonardo, the picture,
Not the Table, I must add, is perhaps most famous
Of them all. Yet again, it is what happens on it that
Gives significance beyond what eyes can perceive.
There, as here, it is what's birthed upon it's surface
That gives the significance. Passover to life giving
Presence seals that moment. So around this table do
Not delay to eat and drink, pausing to clarify what is
Your intent in life, then forward go to change the world.

98. Transformation

I saw the humble sparrow,
In multi-shades of brown,
Transformed to a contender
For a bird of paradise.

His turquoise wings and
Pale blue breast seemed
Far removed from the Creator's
Wish of humility redeemed.

He simply flew across
The sun-drenched pool,
Where hues of blue delight
The senses, invite a dive.

Could I but be transformed
As he, and join the paradise?
But has it not been done, for
Me, and you, and all in Christ?

99. Liturgy I

If I should stand where others before have stood,
By all accounts, I should be called a fool, at least by most.
So why the fear, the uncertainty, the foreboding
Troubling me, as to a self-assigned task I turn?

Newcomer, no expert, uncertain of my ground,
Yet spurred by friendship of one who loves and lives
The Divine Liturgy of the Greek Orthodox variety,
Learning in his later years to sing that which must be sung.

Wanting to learn, to understand, what grips both
Soul and life in unrelenting regular repetition,
Lately, I stood when they stood, sat when they sat,
Said Amen and watched, and watched, wanting more.

I began my exploration with a book and found some
Gems between its gleaming covers: 'Let us Attend',
Penned by one Fr. Lawrence R. Farley, is revelation.
So an ancient meaning of a 'service to the people' changed.

A journey is begun. God's journey to his children,
The children's journey to their God. A Kingdom
Born to be encountered in 'Today', birthed through
The Christ on earth and consummated in His Heaven.

Incorporation, then, for saint and sinner in their
Joint predicament. The broken body shared, in
Which we all partake, reconstitutes resurrection.
Eternal life on the earth begun, heaven continued.

Interaction, interplay, ascending and descending,
Holds the essence. The meeting place of human
And divine made one person in The Christ, now shared
In our humanity, taking us towards divinity. Foretaste.

The pillow caressed my head and thoughts began
A journey, but sight was clearer than beyond my
Memory. A huge plain, delineated by absence of
Undulations but verdant in its colouring, lay below.

Above, a heaven. There is no other name for me
To give the gem-strewn surface, suspended from above,
With what I could not see. It was the in-between,
Capturing attention. Above and below seemed joined.

Disclosure revealed a different truth. Far from
The high, heavenly, rippling surface, distinctiveness
Gave clarity to amassed angelic wings whose gentle
Motion allowed a funnelling down, until only one.

And, from the vast plain, that same distinctiveness
Disclosed humanity. Individuality was well disguised,
As inversion of the funnelling down was now in
The ascending mode, climbing high until, again, only one.
It was this One that became the focus of thought
As well as sight, both human and divine. From this
Angle, he had wings and, from that, a beaten back
Bearing dry, encrusted blood of that bold-red crimson.

Constantly in change of light and shade, movement
Impossible to capture, to hold for less than seconds,
Such a sight beyond capacity to contain in description,

Humanity displaying divinity, divinity displaying humanity.

There, from the myriad of humankind, distilled
To One, between the myriad of angelic hosts likewise
Distilled, to this same One, clothed glory and decay
There. Not standing, yet in light seemingly suspended.

One partakes; the Other subsumes and is subsumed.
This bread, my body broken; this wine, my blood shed.
Overcame my consciousness. What mystery disclosed
As I, in faith, began to eat and drink to satisfy my…what?

Unity. How to describe, how to define the content
Of that word? Impossible, it seemed to me. Only
Experience alone gave insight, leaving a craving for
The moment hardly seen, yet radically imprinted.

Looking on the One, spoken of as Him, consumed
Me. Back to the world, or ascending to some heaven,
It seemed to matter not. Is this the essence, is this
The goal, is this the journey of the Divine Liturgy?

Remade, renewed, reborn. The apostle's declaration.
A New Creation, where the old is no longer and the
New, birthed in life eternal, living out the chores of
Days that are, and days that are to come, not ad infinitum.

Thrice holy, have your mercy on us mortals, Trisagion.
Release to us the Epistle, as we chant the Prokeimenon.
In bringing prayer, encouragement is in Ektenia.
Standing aright from creed, now to the great Anaphora.

Communion climax is the goal as, step by step, the
Journey to the kingdom takes each forward, as
Going forth, the thunderous joy of heaven echoes round
The earth again, as faithful's ears await tomorrow's call.

100. Liturgy II

Liturgy has one grand design, one purpose,
One plan divine: conceived of love before
The birth of time. Of simplicity, sublime.
To get me from where I am to who You are.
You have made your journey that I may make mine.
Your route was incarnation – carpenter to cross.
Thence resurrection, ascension, all to release to me
The Holy Spirit, in gifts and fruit, so I to You
Might come. So, setting out to walk the walk
I'll try, not just to talk the talk. To let Your life,
Through my dead arteries flow for all
Eternity. To find a home in time, and life
Being resurrected in my dying form.

(John 17:10. My glory seen in them)

www.ingramcontent.com/pod-product-compliance
Lightning Source LLC
Chambersburg PA
CBHW070547100426
42744CB00006B/241